Nginx Deep Dive
In-Depth Strategies and Techniques for Mastery

Contents

1 Introduction to Nginx   **11**

  1.1   What is Nginx? 11

  1.2   The History of Nginx 13

  1.3   How Does Nginx Work? 14

  1.4   Key Features of Nginx 16

  1.5   Common Use Cases of Nginx 19

  1.6   Difference Between Nginx and Apache 21

  1.7   Nginx Open Source vs. Nginx Plus 23

  1.8   Basic Nginx Commands 24

  1.9   Understanding Nginx Configuration Files 26

  1.10 Navigating the Nginx Documentation 28

2 Nginx Installation and Configuration   **31**

  2.1   System Requirements for Nginx 31

  2.2   Installing Nginx on Linux 34

  2.3   Installing Nginx on Windows 36

  2.4   Installing Nginx on macOS 37

  2.5   Basic Nginx Configuration Syntax 39

2.6   Configuring Nginx as a Web Server   41

2.7   Testing and Reloading Nginx Configuration   44

2.8   Setting Up Virtual Hosts in Nginx   45

2.9   Enabling HTTPS with SSL/TLS   47

2.10 Directory Structure and Configuration Files   49

2.11 Troubleshooting Common Installation Issues   52

2.12 Upgrading and Uninstalling Nginx   54

3   Understanding Nginx Architecture and Processing Phases   57

3.1   Overview of Nginx Architecture   58

3.2   Event-Driven Model Explained   59

3.3   Worker Processes and Their Roles   61

3.4   Handling Client Requests   63

3.5   The Phases of Request Processing   65

3.6   Understanding Server Blocks and Contexts   67

3.7   Location Blocks: Matching and Processing   70

3.8   Variables and Their Scope   73

3.9   Rewrite Rules and Their Execution   75

3.10 The Role of SSL/TLS in Request Processing   77

3.11 Logging and Error Handling   79

3.12 Optimizing Resource Usage and Performance   80

4   Configuring Web Servers: Domains, SSL, and HTTPS   83

4.1   Domain Name Configuration in Nginx   83

4.2   SSL/TLS Basics for Web Security   86

4.3   Generating SSL Certificates   88

4.4   Configuring Nginx to Use SSL/TLS   90

4.5   Redirecting HTTP Traffic to HTTPS   92

4.6 Working with Let's Encrypt for Free SSL/TLS Certificates 93

4.7 Fine-Tuning SSL/TLS Settings for Enhanced Security 95

4.8 HTTP/2 Support and Configuration 97

4.9 Managing Multiple Domains and Subdomains 99

4.10 Securing Web Applications with Content Security Policies 101

4.11 Performance Considerations for SSL/TLS 103

4.12 Troubleshooting Common SSL/TLS Issues 105

5 Reverse Proxy and Load Balancing   **109**

5.1 Introduction to Reverse Proxying with Nginx 109

5.2 Setting Up Nginx as a Reverse Proxy 111

5.3 Load Balancing Techniques in Nginx 113

5.4 Configuring Upstream Servers for Load Balancing . . 115

5.5 Load Balancing Algorithms and Their Configurations 117

5.6 Health Checks and Failover Strategies 120

5.7 SSL/TLS Termination and Pass-Through 122

5.8 Caching Content from Upstream Servers 125

5.9 WebSocket Reverse Proxying 127

5.10 Restricting Access with Reverse Proxies 129

5.11 Using Variables in Proxy Pass Directives 131

5.12 Troubleshooting Common Reverse Proxy and Load Balancing Issues 133

6 Caching Strategies in Nginx   **137**

6.1 Understanding the Basics of Caching 137

6.2 Types of Caching Available in Nginx 139

6.3   Configuring Static File Caching   141

6.4   Dynamic Content Caching Strategies   143

6.5   Cache Invalidation and Purging Techniques   145

6.6   Setting Up Cache Zones   147

6.7   Controlling Cache with HTTP Headers   149

6.8   Using Proxy Cache for Reverse Proxy Caching   151

6.9   Micro-Caching for Dynamic Content   153

6.10 Integrating Third-Party Caching Tools with Nginx . .   156

6.11 Caching Best Practices   157

6.12 Monitoring and Debugging Cache Performance . . .   159

7   **Securing Nginx: Security Best Practices and Modules**   **163**

7.1   Overview of Web Security and Nginx   164

7.2   Securing Nginx Installation and File Permissions . . .   166

7.3   Using SSL / TLS for Secure Connections   168

7.4   Implementing HTTP Security Headers   170

7.5   Limiting Access with Basic Authentication   172

7.6   Securing Against Brute Force Attacks   173

7.7   Protection Against Web Application Vulnerabilities .   175

7.8   Configuring Nginx Firewalls   178

7.9   Rate Limiting to Prevent Abuse   180

7.10 Logging and Monitoring for Security   182

7.11 Understanding and Using Nginx Security Modules .   184

7.12 Regular Updates and Patch Management   186

8   **Monitoring and Logging with Nginx**   **191**

8.1   Introduction to Monitoring and Logging in Nginx . .   192

8.2   Understanding Nginx Log Files   193

8.3   Configuring Access and Error Logs   195

8.4   Log Rotation and Management   197

8.5   Analyzing Log Files with Third-Party Tools   200

8.6   Real-Time Monitoring Options   202

8.7   Integrating Nginx with External Monitoring Tools . .   204

8.8   Performance Metrics to Monitor in Nginx   207

8.9   Troubleshooting Common Issues with Logs   209

8.10 Security Considerations in Logging   211

8.11 Alerting Based on Log Analysis   214

8.12 Customizing Log Formats for Advanced Analysis . .   216

9   Performance Tuning and Optimization   219

9.1   Basics of Web Performance   219

9.2   Optimizing Nginx Configuration for Speed   222

9.3   Tuning TCP/IP Settings for Performance   224

9.4   Content Compression and Gzip Settings   226

9.5   Caching Strategies for Performance   228

9.6   Load Balancing for High Availability and Performance 231

9.7   SSL/TLS Performance Optimization   233

9.8   Leveraging HTTP/2 for Improved Performance . . .   235

9.9   Fine-Tuning Worker Processes and Connections . . .   237

9.10 Monitoring System Resources for Bottlenecks   239

9.11 Advanced Performance Tools and Techniques   241

10 Advanced Nginx Features and Module Development   245

10.1 Exploring Advanced Nginx Features   245

10.2 Introduction to Nginx Module Development   249

10.3 Types of Modules in Nginx   251

10.4 Setting Up Development Environment for Module Development 253

10.5 Creating a Basic Nginx Module 255

10.6 Understanding Nginx's Internal APIs 258

10.7 Hooking into Nginx's Processing Phases 260

10.8 Config Directives for Custom Modules 261

10.9 Debugging and Testing Nginx Modules 264

10.10 Contributing to the Nginx Community 267

10.11 Integrating Third-Party Modules 269

10.12 Future Directions in Nginx Development 272

Preface

The purpose of this book, "Nginx Deep Dive: In-Depth Strategies and Techniques for Mastery", is to furnish readers with a meticulous and comprehensive understanding of Nginx, one of the leading web servers in the world. This guide aims to empower you with the intricate knowledge and advanced skills required to deploy, configure, and optimize Nginx in a multitude of environments, addressing diverse use cases and challenges.

This book begins by delving into the foundational architecture, installation processes, and initial configuration of Nginx, but it quickly ventures into the realm of complex, nuanced topics crucial for mastery. Readers will explore cutting-edge security strategies, in-depth performance tuning, and sophisticated module development—transforming basic server management skills into robust, strategic web server expertise. Each chapter is methodically designed to build upon its predecessor, ensuring a logical progression that enables readers to understand both the basic and advanced functionalities of Nginx fluently.

We will also delve into real-world use cases, offering detailed scenarios and step-by-step guides that demonstrate how to harness the full potential of Nginx. This includes its usage as a reverse proxy, load balancer, and as a critical component in a microservices architecture. By thoroughly exploring these advanced capabilities, the book provides an enriched learning path geared towards readers keen on mastering this powerful and versatile software.

The intended audience for this book includes developers, system administrators, DevOps engineers, and any tech-savvy individuals with an interest in web technologies and performance optimization. Whether you are a beginner to Nginx or an experienced user striving to deepen your understanding and expand your expertise, this guide is crafted to enrich your technical arsenal. While a basic understanding of web servers and general web technologies is assumed, prior experience with Nginx, though beneficial, is not required.

This book aspires to be an essential tool in your professional development, offering insights, strategies, and practical knowledge that applies to contemporary challenges and future-oriented scenarios. By the end of this guide, you will possess a profound understanding of Nginx's intricacies and know how to leverage them effectively to enhance the performance, reliability, and security of your web applications.

Our commitment is to deliver a precise, insightful, and hands-on resource that exceeds the needs of professionals aiming to refine their expertise in web server management with Nginx. Your engagement with this book will endow you with the competence necessary to make informed decisions, expertly navigate troubleshooting processes, and implement best practices within your web server environments, ensuring your readiness to tackle both current and emerging technological challenges.

Chapter 1

Introduction to Nginx

Nginx, pronounced as "Engine-X", is a powerful open-source web server software known for its high performance, stability, rich feature set, and low resource consumption. Initially created to solve the C10k problem, it has evolved to offer a fully-fledged web serving, reverse proxying, caching, load balancing, and media streaming. Serving a significant portion of internet traffic today, Nginx stands out for its efficient handling of concurrent connections and its ability to scale dynamically across many environments, from small scale projects to enterprise-level deployments.

1.1   What is Nginx?

Nginx (pronounced as "Engine-X") represents a high-performance, open-source web server software designed to handle a large number of simultaneous connections with minimal resource usage. Beyond serving HTTP web pages, Nginx is renowned for its multipurpose capabilities, including reverse proxying, caching, load balancing, and media streaming. Its architecture is event-driven, enabling efficient handling of numerous concurrent client connections, a stark contrast to traditional thread-based handling models.

Developed by Igor Sysoev in 2002, Nginx was initially conceived to address the C10k challenge, which relates to managing ten thousand concurrent connections. The software quickly gained popularity, owing to its outstanding performance, stability, and low resource requirements. Today, it powers a significant percentage of websites across the internet, being a fundamental component in modern web applications and service infrastructures.

The core functionality of Nginx revolves around serving and routing HTTP requests. It operates as a web server by delivering HTML files and other static content directly to clients. When configured as a reverse proxy, Nginx accepts connections from clients, forwarding requests to backend servers and returning the responses to the clients, acting as an intermediary that can also provide additional layers of control and security.

Moreover, Nginx enhances website performance through its caching capabilities. It can store copies of web pages served, substantially reducing the need to regenerate or fetch these pages from the backend servers on subsequent requests. This caching mechanism is instrumental in reducing server load and improving response times for end-users.

Load balancing is another pivotal feature, enabling Nginx to distribute incoming network traffic across several backend servers. This distribution ensures that no single server becomes a bottleneck, enhancing the reliability and scalability of web applications. It supports various load balancing methods, such as round-robin, least connections, and IP hash, each suitable for different types of workloads and deployment scenarios.

Nginx also offers powerful media streaming functionalities, capable of handling live streaming and video-on-demand efficiently. This makes it an excellent choice for platforms requiring the streaming of audio or video content.

Here is an example of a simple Nginx configuration file snippet that serves static content:

```
server {
    listen 80;
    server_name example.com;
```

```
4
5      location / {
6          root /usr/share/nginx/html;
7          index index.html index.htm;
8      }
9  }
```

This configuration directs Nginx to listen for HTTP requests on port 80 for a server named example.com. It also specifies that requests to the root URL path should be served static content from the specified root directory, with index.html or index.htm as the default files to serve.

The versatility, efficiency, and robust feature set of Nginx make it an indispensable tool in the modern web technology stack, suitable for a myriad of deployments ranging from small scale projects to large, complex enterprise environments.

1.2   The History of Nginx

Nginx, pronounced as "Engine-X," was first conceptualized and developed by Igor Sysoev in the early 2000s. At that time, Sysoev was facing challenges related to the C10k problem, which concerns the difficulty for web server software to handle 10,000 concurrent connections. This problem was particularly acute due to the limitations of traditional web server software architectures, which struggled under the heavy load of modern web traffic.

The primary motivation behind the creation of Nginx was to develop a web server that could solve this problem by using an asynchronous, event-driven architecture. Unlike traditional web servers that spawned new processes or threads for each web request, Nginx's architecture allowed for handling multiple requests within a single thread. This innovation significantly reduced the resources needed to handle high volumes of concurrent connections, thus addressing the C10k problem effectively.

Nginx was officially released to the public in October 2004. Since its initial release, Nginx has evolved from a simple web server into a powerful suite of products. These include Nginx Open Source, the original product, and Nginx Plus, a commercial offering that includes additional features and support.

Over the years, Nginx's performance and efficiency in handling high levels of concurrent traffic have made it a popular choice among web administrators and developers. Its use has grown rapidly, with Nginx now powering many of the world's most heavily trafficked sites.

One of the pivotal moments in Nginx's history came in 2011, when the Nginx, Inc. was founded to provide commercial support and services for Nginx. This move helped accelerate the development of new features and the expansion of Nginx's capabilities beyond serving static content. Features such as reverse proxy, load balancing, caching, and SSL termination were added, making Nginx a powerful all-around solution for web infrastructure needs.

In March 2019, F5 Networks announced its acquisition of Nginx, Inc. for $670 million. This acquisition marked a new chapter in the history of Nginx, bringing additional resources and support to further innovate and expand its offerings.

Throughout its history, Nginx has made a significant impact on the way web servers are built and managed. It has introduced a shift towards efficiency and scalability in web infrastructure, influencing not only how websites and applications are served but also how they are designed and developed. As the internet continues to grow and evolve, Nginx's flexible and efficient architecture ensures that it remains at the forefront of web server technology.

1.3   How Does Nginx Work?

Nginx operates on an event-driven architecture, distinguishing itself significantly from the process-driven or threaded approaches of many other web servers. This model is essential for understanding the efficiency and scalability that Nginx brings to handling high volumes of concurrent connections.

In a typical process or thread-based server model, each incoming connection requires a new process or thread, consuming significant system resources. This setup results in high memory and CPU usage, especially under heavy loads, leading to decreased performance and, in some cases, server unavailability.

Conversely, Nginx utilizes a master-worker architecture that capitalizes on the non-blocking, event-driven approach. This architecture comprises one master process and multiple worker processes. The master process is responsible for reading and validating configuration files, managing worker processes, and performing administrative tasks. It does not handle client requests directly. Once the master process has initialized settings and started the worker processes, its main job is to oversee the general functioning of the server.

Worker processes handle client requests. One of the key features of Nginx is that a single worker process can manage thousands of concurrent connections thanks to its non-blocking I/O operations. This capability stems from the effective use of an asynchronous, event-driven model.

- Non-blocking I/O Operations: Unlike blocking I/O, where a process might wait for an operation to complete, non-blocking I/O allows a single process to issue a request and move on to handle other tasks. When the operation is complete, the process can access the result without having wasted resources waiting.

- Asynchronous Events: Events such as receiving a new connection or completing a data transfer do not block processes. Instead, these events are queued and handled as resources become available, ensuring that each worker can manage multiple connections simultaneously.

Under the hood, Nginx uses the epoll interface on Linux systems, kqueue on BSD-based systems, and other appropriate event notification mechanisms on different operating systems to efficiently detect and respond to events across thousands of connections.

The efficiency of this model lies in its ability to serve a large number of requests with a minimal hardware footprint, making Nginx ideally suited for high traffic websites and applications.

15

```
1    # Example showing non-blocking I/O operation in pseudo-code
2
3    request = receive_non_blocking_io_operation()
4    while (not request.is_complete()):
5        # Perform other tasks while waiting for the operation to complete
6        continue_processing_other_tasks()
7    process_completed_request(request)
```

This pseudo-code illustrates the essence of non-blocking I/O operations, a principle at the core of Nginx's operation. By not waiting for operations to complete before moving on to other tasks, Nginx keeps resource usage low and performance high, even under significant loads.

```
Output example illustrating efficient resource usage:

Processes: 4
Worker Connections: 1024
Total Connections Handled: 4096
System Memory Usage: Minimal
```

Conclusively, the event-driven, asynchronous model of Nginx allows it to efficiently handle a vast number of concurrent connections, making it an optimal choice for modern web applications demanding high performance and scalability.

1.4   Key Features of Nginx

Nginx, standing at the forefront of web server technologies, offers an extensive array of features that contribute to its widespread adoption and favorability among system administrators and developers alike. The architecture of Nginx is fundamentally designed to excel in speed, efficiency, and reliability, making it a viable choice for a broad spectrum of web applications. In this section, we will discuss the fundamental characteristics that distinguish Nginx from other web servers.

Event-Driven Architecture

One of the primary features that set Nginx apart is its event-driven architecture. Unlike traditional web servers that create a new thread for each incoming request, leading to substantial overhead and increased resource usage, Nginx operates on an asynchronous, non-blocking model. This means that a single worker process can handle thousands of connections concurrently, contributing significantly to its efficiency and scalability. The event-driven model allows Nginx to provide high performance while consuming minimal system resources.

Reverse Proxy and Load Balancing

Nginx is widely recognized for its capability to serve as a reverse proxy and load balancer. As a reverse proxy, Nginx can manage requests from clients, forwarding them to other servers for processing and then returning the responses back to the clients. This feature enables various use cases, including providing a unified front-end for multiple application servers, enhancing security by obscuring the identities of backend servers, and facilitating SSL termination.

Regarding load balancing, Nginx supports a variety of algorithms, such as round-robin, least-connected, and IP-hash, among others. This functionality allows for the efficient distribution of client requests across multiple backend servers, ensuring optimal resource utilization and minimizing response times. Load balancing also improves application availability and reliability by enabling failover among servers.

High Performance Static Content Serving

Nginx excels at serving static content with unparalleled efficiency. By leveraging an optimized handling of static resources, such as images, CSS, and JavaScript files, Nginx can deliver content at an impressive speed. This is achieved through techniques such as

17

direct file serving from the cache, minimizing disk read operations, and employing sendfile, tcp_nodelay, and tcp_nopush settings. Consequently, websites and applications behind Nginx experience faster loading times, a crucial factor for user satisfaction and SEO rankings.

Caching

Caching is another key feature of Nginx, allowing frequently accessed content to be stored temporarily in memory. This reduces the need to generate dynamic content or retrieve static content from disk for each request, leading to a significant decrease in response times and server load. Nginx provides extensive control over caching behavior, including cache validation, expiration, and bypass mechanisms. Effective caching strategies enhance the performance and scalability of web applications by minimizing the processing overhead on backend servers.

Security Features

Nginx incorporates a variety of security features to safeguard web applications from common threats and attacks. Among these features are the ability to restrict access based on client IP addresses, password authentication for protected areas, and rate limiting to mitigate the effects of traffic spikes or denial-of-service attacks. Additionally, Nginx supports SSL/TLS for encrypted client-server communication, helping to ensure the confidentiality and integrity of data in transit.

Flexible Configuration System

The configuration system of Nginx is both powerful and flexible, offering granular control over the web server's operation. Configurations in Nginx are structured in a hierarchical manner, with directives organized into blocks that define the behavior of the server, virtual hosts, locations, and other components. This structure facilitates straightforward management of complex configurations and enables precise tuning of server performance, security, and functionality.

The key features of Nginx—its event-driven architecture, reverse proxy capabilities, load balancing, efficient static content serving, caching, security mechanisms, and flexible configuration system—collectively contribute to its reputation as a robust, high-performance web server suited for a wide range of applications. Whether deployed in small-scale projects or large enterprise environments, Nginx consistently demonstrates its ability to handle high traffic volumes while optimizing resource usage and enhancing application responsiveness.

1.5 Common Use Cases of Nginx

Nginx, recognized for its versatility and performance, is widely utilized in various capacities across the internet. Below, we will explore some of the most prevalent use cases of Nginx, demonstrating its flexibility and efficiency in handling different web-serving needs.

- **Web Serving:** At its core, Nginx is a web server. It efficiently serves static content, such as HTML, CSS, and JavaScript files, by directly delivering them to clients without the need for additional processing. This inherent efficiency is attributable to Nginx's asynchronous, event-driven architecture, significantly reducing the resources required to serve multiple concurrent requests.

- **Reverse Proxy and Load Balancing:** Nginx is frequently deployed as a reverse proxy and load balancer. In this setup, Nginx acts as an intermediary for requests from clients seeking resources from backend servers. This configuration enables Nginx to distribute incoming traffic across multiple servers, enhancing the responsiveness and reliability of web applications by distributing the load, reducing the strain on individual servers, and ensuring that applications remain available even if one or more servers become overloaded or fail.

- **Caching:** Caching is another critical capability of Nginx, wherein frequently requested resources are stored temporarily in a cache. Subsequent requests for these resources can be served directly from the cache, significantly reducing the load on the backend servers and accelerating the response time to the client. This feature is especially beneficial for dynamic websites with high traffic, where identical content is repeatedly requested.

- **Media Streaming:** Nginx is also capable of handling live streaming and video-on-demand services. By utilizing Nginx's HTTP Live Streaming (HLS) and HTTP Dynamic Streaming (HDS) modules, developers can efficiently stream audio and video content to clients in various formats, adjusting the quality dynamically based on the client's bandwidth.

- **Security and Anonymity:** Nginx plays a pivotal role in enhancing the security and privacy of web applications. It can be configured to authenticate incoming requests, encrypt data using SSL/TLS protocols, and serve as an anonymizing reverse proxy that hides the identities of underlying servers. This multifaceted approach significantly augments the security posture of web applications by mitigating the risk of malicious attacks and data breaches.

The versatility of Nginx is evident from its wide range of applications, from serving simple static websites to acting as the backbone for complex, high-traffic web applications. This adaptability, coupled with its efficiency and reliability, makes Nginx an indispensable tool in the modern web ecosystem.

1.6   Difference Between Nginx and Apache

Nginx and Apache are both powerful and popular web servers, each with its unique set of features and operational differences. Understanding the distinctions between the two can help in making an informed decision based on the specific requirements of a project.

Apache, developed by the Apache Software Foundation, has been a dominant web server since its inception in 1995. It operates on a process-driven architecture where each request creates a new thread or process, potentially leading to significant resource consumption under heavy loads. This design, although robust and fully-featured, sometimes struggles with a high number of simultaneous connections.

On the other hand, Nginx (pronounced "Engine-X") was created by Igor Sysoev in 2004 with the specific goal of addressing the C10k problem, which involves efficiently handling 10,000 concurrent connections. Nginx employs an event-driven architecture, making it highly scalable and efficient in managing multiple connections due to a non-blocking, asynchronous approach. This architecture minimizes the use of resources and enables Nginx to serve a large number of requests simultaneously without creating new processes for each.

The key differences between Nginx and Apache can be summarized in the following points:

- **Architecture:** Apache uses a process-driven or thread-driven architecture, while Nginx uses an event-driven model, leading to lower memory consumption and increased capacity for handling concurrent connections.

- **Performance:** Under high concurrency scenarios, Nginx is generally observed to perform better due to its efficient use of system resources. Apache, however, might perform comparably or even better under conditions with less concurrency due to its ability to leverage a wide range of dynamic modules.

- **Configuration:** Apache's configuration system is highly flexi-

ble, allowing for .htaccess files and direct configuration directives, making it easier for per-directory configurations without
server restart. Nginx, in contrast, does not support .htaccess
files, requiring all configurations to be done in the main configuration file and necessitating a restart or reload of the server to
apply changes.

- **Content:**   Apache is known for its strong support for
  dynamically generated content through embedded interpreter
  support for scripting languages directly within the web server.
  Nginx, traditionally, was designed as a reverse proxy server
  and excels in serving static content quickly; for dynamic
  content, it generally proxies requests to a backend server
  running a separate interpreter.

- **Modules:**   Both servers support modular architectures,
  however, Apache offers a wider range of dynamic modules,
  allowing for on-the-fly inclusion and exclusion without
  restarting the server. Nginx modules, while also plentiful,
  need to be selected and compiled into the server binary at
  build time.

These distinctions highlight that the choice between Nginx and
Apache largely depends on the specific needs of an application. For
projects requiring scalability and efficient management of a high
number of concurrent connections, Nginx may be the preferred
choice. In contrast, Apache might be more suitable for applications
that benefit from its comprehensive support for dynamically
generated content and its extensive range of modules.

Choosing between Nginx and Apache requires an understanding of
the application's needs regarding performance, scalability, and the
type of content served. Both web servers have proven their reliability and performance across various environments, and the decision
should be based on the criteria most critical to the project's success.

1.7 Nginx Open Source vs. Nginx Plus

Nginx is available in two primary flavors: the open-source version and Nginx Plus, the commercial version. The open-source variant is widely used and is sufficient for a broad range of web serving and proxy needs. Nginx Plus, on the other hand, is tailored towards enterprise usage, offering additional features, support, and services not found in the open-source version.

- **Features:** The open-source version of Nginx includes core web serving, reverse proxying, caching, and basic load balancing capabilities. Nginx Plus extends these capabilities with advanced features such as active health checks, session persistence, DNS-based service discovery, and a comprehensive monitoring and management dashboard.

- **Support and Services:** While the open-source version relies on community support, Nginx Plus provides professional support directly from the developers of Nginx. This support includes technical assistance, troubleshooting, and help with configuration issues. Additionally, Nginx Plus customers have access to regular software updates and security patches.

- **Performance and Scalability:** Both versions are built on the same core, offering high performance and efficient handling of concurrent connections. However, Nginx Plus includes performance enhancements and scalability features tailored to large-scale deployments, such as adaptive media streaming and enhanced load balancing algorithms.

- **Security:** Nginx Plus comes with advanced security features, including JWT authentication, access control based on JWT claims, and integration with external authentication systems. While the open-source version supports basic security measures, Nginx Plus provides a more comprehensive security solution.

The choice between Nginx open source and Nginx Plus depends on the specific needs of the deployment. For small to medium-sized projects or those with limited budgets, the open-source version often suffices. However, enterprise-level deployments that require advanced features, professional support, and enhanced security may find Nginx Plus to be a more suitable choice.

```
1   # Sample NGINX configuration snippet showing basic server block
2   server {
3       listen 80;
4       server_name example.com;
5
6       location / {
7           root /var/www/html;
8           index index.html index.htm;
9       }
10  }
```

The snippet above illustrates a basic server configuration in Nginx open-source version. Configuring Nginx involves defining server blocks within the Nginx configuration files. These blocks dictate how incoming requests are handled and processed.

```
Welcome to nginx!
If you see this page, the nginx web server is successfully installed and working.
```

The output above appears when accessing the root URL of a server running Nginx after a successful installation. It indicates that Nginx is correctly handling HTTP requests.

While the open-source version of Nginx provides a robust set of features suitable for many web serving and proxying tasks, Nginx Plus offers additional advanced features, professional support, and services designed for business-critical enterprise environments.

1.8   Basic Nginx Commands

In this section, we will discuss essential Nginx commands that are crucial for managing the Nginx server. These commands allow administrators and developers to start, stop, and control the Nginx server efficiently. Familiarity with these commands can greatly improve one's ability to work with Nginx and troubleshoot potential issues.

- `nginx` - This command starts the Nginx server. Executing this command without any options will launch Nginx by reading the   default   configuration   file   located   at `/etc/nginx/nginx.conf`. This is typically the first command used after installing Nginx.

- `nginx -s stop` - This command immediately stops the Nginx server. It does not wait for the currently processing requests to finish before stopping the service. This command is useful when you need to quickly stop all Nginx activities due to, for example, a critical configuration error or security issue.

- `nginx -s quit` - This command gracefully stops the Nginx server. Unlike the `stop` signal, `quit` waits for Nginx to complete processing all active requests before shutting down. This command is preferred for routine maintenance and server restarts to ensure no disruption to client requests.

- `nginx -s reload` - This command reloads the Nginx configuration file without stopping the server. The main use case for this command is applying configuration changes without interrupting the current client connections. It is especially valuable in environments where minimizing downtime is crucial.

- `nginx -t` - Before applying changes with the reload command, it is best practice to test the Nginx configuration files for syntax errors. The `nginx -t` command checks the syntax of the configuration file and outputs any errors, allowing for correction before applying changes that could potentially disrupt service.

- `nginx -v` - This command displays the version of the Nginx server currently installed on the system. Knowing the version is   important   when   troubleshooting,   referencing documentation, or when determining compatibility with Nginx modules or third-party dependencies.

When troubleshooting or configuring the Nginx server, it may be helpful to observe the logs generated by Nginx. The following commands facilitate viewing and managing these logs:

- **Access log viewing**: The command `tail -f /var/log/nginx/access.log` can be used to view incoming requests in real-time. This is vital for monitoring the traffic being handled by Nginx.

- **Error log viewing**: To check for errors, the command `tail -f /var/log/nginx/error.log` is used. Real-time monitoring of this log can provide immediate insights into issues affecting the Nginx server or hosted applications.

These commands form the foundation of managing and troubleshooting an Nginx server. Proper understanding and usage can significantly enhance the ability to maintain high availability and performance of hosted applications.

1.9 Understanding Nginx Configuration Files

Understanding the structure and syntax of Nginx configuration files is crucial for effectively managing and optimizing Nginx as a web server. Nginx configuration files are written in a straightforward, human-readable format and define how the server processes requests. These files are typically located in the `/etc/nginx` directory on a Unix-like system. The main configuration file is `nginx.conf`, which may include additional configuration files to organize settings for specific modules or sites.

Nginx interprets the configuration directives in a hierarchical context structure, including `main`, `http`, `server`, and `location` contexts. Each context supports a set of directives specific to its operational scope which allows for granular control over Nginx's behavior.

```
1   # Example of an Nginx configuration structure
2   http {
3       server {
4           listen 80;
5           server_name example.com;
6
```

```
 7         location / {
 8             root /var/www/html;
 9             index index.html index.htm;
10         }
11     }
12 }
```

The `http` context configures directives that apply to HTTP and HTTPS protocols. Within the `http` context, the `server` blocks define server-specific configurations. Each `server` block can host a website or an application, identifying itself using the `listen` and `server_name` directives. The `location` blocks within a `server` context specify how to process requests to different resources.

Directives within Nginx configuration files can reference variables, which offer dynamic values based on request or server properties. This capability supports flexible and powerful configurations, such as conditional behaviors or custom logging formats.

```
1 log_format main '$remote_addr - $remote_user [$time_local] "$request" '
2                  '$status $body_bytes_sent "$http_referer" '
3                  '"$http_user_agent" "$http_x_forwarded_for"';
```

Nginx configuration files support the inclusion of other files using the `include` directive. This feature facilitates modular configuration approaches, allowing administrators to maintain common settings or virtual host configurations separately.

```
1 include /etc/nginx/conf.d/*.conf;
```

After modifying Nginx configurations, it is good practice to validate the configurations for syntax errors before applying them. Use the Nginx command-line utility with the `-t` flag to perform this check, as shown below.

```
1 nginx -t
```

```
nginx: the configuration file /etc/nginx/nginx.conf syntax is ok
nginx: configuration file /etc/nginx/nginx.conf test is successful
```

Lastly, understanding the principles of operation and the logical structure behind Nginx configuration files is fundamental to leveraging its full potential. Effective use of contexts, directives,

27

and inclusion patterns can significantly optimize web server performance and scalability.

1.10   Navigating the Nginx Documentation

Accessing accurate and detailed documentation is crucial for effectively working with Nginx, whether for setting up a server, troubleshooting, or optimizing performance. The official Nginx documentation is a comprehensive resource that provides guidelines, references, and examples. This section will focus on strategies for efficiently finding and utilizing the information within the Nginx documentation.

First, it's important to understand how the Nginx documentation is organized. The main categories include:

- Installation and Basic Usage: Guides on installing Nginx on various operating systems and the basic commands to start, stop, and manage Nginx services.

- Beginner's Guide: A step-by-step guide designed for users who are new to Nginx.

- Admin Guide: Covers more advanced topics such as configuration, security, logging, and module management.

- Developer Documentation: Provides information for developers who are interested in contributing to the Nginx codebase or developing Nginx modules.

- Directive Dictionary: Lists all the directives that can be used in Nginx configuration files, grouped by modules.

- Example Configurations: Contains practical examples of Nginx configurations for different scenarios.

To effectively navigate the documentation, it's recommended to start with the "Beginner's Guide" if you are new to Nginx. This guide will provide you with the foundational knowledge required to move on to more complex topics. Once you have a grasp of the basics, the "Admin Guide" becomes a valuable resource for understanding the nuances of Nginx administration and optimization.

For specific configuration needs or to understand what directives are available for use, consulting the "Directive Dictionary" is essential. This section is particularly helpful when customizing your Nginx server to meet precise requirements. It's organized by module, making it easier to find the directives related to the functionality you are configuring, such as caching, load balancing, or security.

When encountering issues or implementing a new feature, the "Example Configurations" section can be an invaluable resource. Seeing real-world examples can provide insights and inspiration for your own configurations. Additionally, should you need to troubleshoot an issue or optimize performance, the "Admin Guide" offers detailed discussions on logging, monitoring, and performance tuning.

For developers interested in contributing to Nginx or creating custom modules, the "Developer Documentation" provides the necessary guidelines and reference materials. This includes information on the development environment, coding standards, and how to submit contributions.

Lastly, navigating the Nginx documentation efficiently requires the use of its search functionality. The documentation website includes a search bar that can quickly direct you to the relevant sections or topics. Utilizing keywords related to your query can significantly reduce the time spent looking for information.

Here is an example of a common query one might have regarding Nginx configuration files:

```
1  # Redirect HTTP to HTTPS
2  server {
3      listen 80;
4      server_name example.com www.example.com;
5      return 301 https://$server_name$request_uri;
6  }
```

The above configuration snippet demonstrates a basic redirect from HTTP to HTTPS, which is a common requirement for web applications. Detailed explanations of each directive used in this snippet can be found in the "Directive Dictionary".

Effectively navigating the Nginx documentation involves understanding its structure, starting with guides aligned with your knowledge level, using the "Directive Dictionary" for reference, examining "Example Configurations" for practical applications, and leveraging the search functionality for precise queries. With these strategies, you can efficiently find the information needed to successfully work with Nginx.

Chapter 2

Nginx Installation and Configuration

Installing and configuring Nginx involves a straightforward set of steps tailored to various operating systems. Through its flexible configuration system, Nginx allows users to finely tune server behavior to fit specific needs. This process includes setting up Nginx as a web server, configuring it to serve static and dynamic content, securing connections with SSL/TLS, and optimizing its performance. The initial setup lays the groundwork for further customization and optimization, ensuring Nginx runs efficiently and securely as part of a larger network infrastructure.

2.1 System Requirements for Nginx

Installing Nginx requires an understanding of the minimal system requirements to ensure efficient operation. These requirements vary based on the workload, the number of concurrent connections expected, and the complexity of the tasks Nginx is expected to perform. Generally, Nginx is designed to be lightweight and can run on systems with limited resources, but optimizing performance might necessitate more substantial hardware.

Hardware Requirements

- **CPU:** The processing power needed by Nginx primarily depends on the nature of the tasks. For a basic setup serving static content, a single-core processor can suffice. However, for dynamic content, SSL/TLS encryption, or high traffic sites, multiple CPU cores are recommended to handle concurrent connections efficiently.

- **Memory (RAM):** Nginx itself requires minimal memory; however, the total amount of RAM needed is influenced by the size of the content being served, caching configurations, and the number of active connections. As a baseline, 512MB of RAM can support a low-traffic website, but 1-2GB or more may be necessary for higher demands.

- **Disk Space:** While Nginx's executable files take up minimal space, sufficient disk space must be allocated for logs, site content, and temporary files used for caching. The starting point can be as low as 50MB for Nginx itself, but significantly more is required for content and operational data, easily reaching GBs in a busy server environment.

- **Network Interface:** The required network bandwidth is contingent upon the expected traffic. Gigabit Ethernet (1Gbps) is standard in most scenarios, but higher-speed interfaces may be beneficial for very high traffic sites.

Software Requirements

Nginx can be installed on a variety of operating systems, including Linux, Windows, and macOS. The choice of the operating system might depend on the user's familiarity, the specific requirements of other software components, or the hosting environment's constraints.

- **Linux:** Most Linux distributions are supported, including Ubuntu, CentOS, Debian, and Red Hat Enterprise Linux. A minimal installation is sufficient, as Nginx does not require a graphical user interface (GUI).

- **Windows:** Nginx runs on Windows, though it's more commonly deployed on Linux for production environments. It supports Windows Server 2012, 2016, and newer versions, along with Windows 10 for development purposes.

- **macOS:** While not a common production environment for Nginx, macOS can provide a comfortable development setup for those accustomed to the platform. Nginx works on the most recent versions of macOS.

Network Considerations

- A dedicated or virtual private server (VPS) is recommended for hosting Nginx, especially for public-facing websites, to provide adequate resources and security isolation.

- Ensure that the server's firewall is configured to allow traffic on the ports that Nginx will use, typically port 80 for HTTP and port 443 for HTTPS.

- Configuring network complexities such as reverse proxy setups, load balancing, or integrating with a content delivery network (CDN) might require advanced network interface configurations and increased bandwidth.

Understanding and meeting these system requirements before installation will lay a foundation for a smoothly running Nginx server. Each deployment should be assessed individually, taking into account the particular use case and traffic expectations, to fine-tune these recommendations to the specific scenario.

2.2   Installing Nginx on Linux

Installing Nginx on a Linux system is a straightforward process that involves a series of commands executed in the terminal. This section will guide you through the necessary steps to download and install Nginx on various Linux distributions, such as Ubuntu, Debian, CentOS, and Fedora. Each distribution has its own package management system, and we'll cover the methods applicable to each.

Ubuntu and Debian

For Ubuntu and Debian systems, Nginx is available in the default repositories, and the installation can be performed using the apt package manager. First, it is recommended to update the package repository index to ensure you are installing the latest version of Nginx available. The following commands achieve this:

```
1   sudo apt update
2   sudo apt install nginx
```

After the installation process is complete, Nginx will start automatically. To verify that Nginx is running, you can use the following command:

```
1   sudo systemctl status nginx
```

If Nginx is running correctly, you should see output indicating that the service is active.

CentOS and Fedora

On CentOS and Fedora, Nginx is not available in the default repositories but can be installed from the EPEL (Extra Packages for Enterprise Linux) repository. First, install the EPEL repository with the following command:

```
1   sudo yum install epel-release
```

Once the EPEL repository is installed, you can install Nginx using yum (CentOS) or dnf (Fedora) as follows:

For CentOS:

```
1  sudo yum install nginx
```

For Fedora:

```
1  sudo dnf install nginx
```

After the installation is complete, you need to start Nginx and enable it to launch at boot using the following commands:

```
1  sudo systemctl start nginx
2  sudo systemctl enable nginx
```

To confirm that Nginx has been successfully started, you can run:

```
1  sudo systemctl status nginx
```

You should see output similar to the Ubuntu and Debian section, indicating that Nginx is active and running.

General Configuration and Verification

Regardless of the Linux distribution, once Nginx is installed, you can verify that it is correctly serving pages by navigating to the server's IP address or domain name in a web browser. By default, Nginx serves a welcome page on port 80, which confirms the web server is correctly installed and operational.

To verify from the command line, you can use the curl command:

```
1  curl http://localhost
```

The output should include HTML code from Nginx's default welcome page:

```
<!DOCTYPE html>
<html>
<head>
<title>Welcome to nginx!</title>
...
```

35

```
</html>
```

This indicates that Nginx is correctly installed and operational on your Linux system. Following the installation, you may proceed to configure Nginx to serve your web content by editing its configuration files, a process that will be covered in subsequent sections.

2.3   Installing Nginx on Windows

Installing Nginx on a Windows operating system requires a different set of steps when compared to Linux or macOS, due to the inherent differences in the operating systems' environments and file management systems. The following guidance ensures a smooth installation process, preparing the system for further configuration and optimization tasks.

First, it is important to download the correct version of Nginx for Windows. Visit the official Nginx website (`http://nginx.org/en/download.html`) and navigate to the Windows versions. Select the appropriate version for your system. While Nginx is primarily developed for Unix-like systems, a version for Windows is available, usually indicated as "nginx/Windows".

- Download the latest stable version of Nginx for Windows.

- Save the downloaded zip file to a directory on your Windows system where you wish to run Nginx from. It is recommended to choose a location that's easily accessible, such as `C:\nginx`.

After the file has been downloaded, follow these steps to extract and run Nginx:

1. Navigate to the directory where you downloaded the Nginx zip file.

2. Right-click on the zip file and choose "Extract All..." to unzip the contents. Ensure that the target destination is as intended (e.g., C:\nginx).

3. Open the extracted directory, then navigate into the newly created directory until you find the executable file named nginx.exe.

4. Double-click nginx.exe to run Nginx. There won't be any visible window indicating that Nginx is running; however, Nginx will start serving content on port 80 by default.

To confirm that Nginx is successfully running on your Windows system, open a web browser and enter the URL http://localhost. You should be greeted with the default Nginx welcome page. If you see this page, it indicates that Nginx has been installed and is running correctly.

Managing the Nginx server process on Windows can be done directly from the command prompt. To do this, open a command prompt and navigate to the directory where nginx.exe is located. You can manage the Nginx process using the following commands:

```
1  nginx -s stop # Fast shutdown
2  nginx -s quit # Graceful shutdown
3  nginx -s reload # Reload the configuration file
4  nginx -s reopen # Reopen log files
```

For a more persistent setup, you may want to add Nginx to Windows' Service Management so that Nginx automatically starts with Windows. However, this requires additional software, such as WinSW, to create a Windows service wrapper for nginx.exe.

Installing Nginx on Windows involves downloading the correct version from the official website, extracting the files to a preferred location, and running nginx.exe. Upon successful installation, Nginx will serve content on port 80, with its management facilitated through specific commands executed in the command prompt.

2.4   Installing Nginx on macOS

Installing Nginx on macOS can be accomplished through multiple methods, but the most straightforward and efficient approach is using Homebrew, a popular package manager for macOS. This section will guide you through the installation process using Homebrew, as well as cover basic steps to ensure the web server is running properly.

Pre-requisites

Before installing Nginx, ensure that Homebrew is installed on your macOS system. If Homebrew is not already installed, it can be easily set up by executing the following command in the terminal:

```
1   /bin/bash -c "$(curl -fsSL https://raw.githubusercontent.com/Homebrew/install/
        master/install.sh)"
```

This command downloads the Homebrew installation script and executes it.

Installing Nginx

With Homebrew installed, you can proceed to install Nginx. To do so, open your terminal and execute the following command:

```
1   brew install nginx
```

This command fetches the latest version of Nginx and installs it on your system. The process may take a few minutes depending on your internet connection speed. Once the installation is complete, you can verify that Nginx has been installed properly by checking its version:

```
1   nginx -v
```

The output should display the installed version of Nginx, confirming that the web server is successfully installed on your machine:

```
nginx version: nginx/1.xx.x
```

Starting Nginx

After installation, you can start the Nginx service using Homebrew services. Execute the following command in your terminal:

```
1  brew services start nginx
```

This command instructs Homebrew to start the Nginx service. By default, Nginx runs on port 8080 on macOS. You can verify that Nginx is running by accessing http://localhost:8080 in your web browser. If Nginx is running properly, you will see the default Nginx welcome page.

Customizing Configuration

Nginx configuration files are located in /usr/local/etc/nginx/. The main configuration file is nginx.conf. You can edit this file to customize server settings, such as changing the default port or setting up virtual hosts. Ensure to reload the Nginx configuration for changes to take effect:

```
1  brew services restart nginx
```

Installing Nginx on macOS using Homebrew is a simple and effective method. Once installed, Nginx can be easily started, stopped, and managed through Homebrew services. Additionally, Nginx's configuration can be customized to meet specific requirements by editing the nginx.conf file. Following the steps outlined in this section should provide a smooth setup experience, readying Nginx for further configuration and optimization according to your project's needs.

2.5 Basic Nginx Configuration Syntax

Nginx utilizes a text-based configuration format that is designed to be straightforward and human-readable. The configuration files are structured using simple directives placed in blocks, which dictate how Nginx should handle incoming requests. Understanding the basic syntax and structure of Nginx configuration files is fundamental for effective server management and optimization.

Directives and Blocks are the primary elements of Nginx's configuration:

- **Directives:** Basic instructions that define how to handle various tasks. Each directive consists of a name and parameters separated by spaces, ending with a semicolon (;). An example of a directive that listens on port 80 is `listen 80;`.

- **Blocks:** Container elements that group related directives. Blocks are defined using curly braces ({}). An example is the `server` block, which contains directives related to the server configuration.

The Nginx configuration file consists of hierarchical blocks, where the `http` block can include multiple `server` blocks, and `server` blocks can include multiple `location` blocks. This hierarchy allows for detailed and nuanced configurations.

```
http {
    server {
        listen 80;
        server_name example.com;

        location / {
            root /var/www/html;
            index index.html index.htm;
        }
    }
}
```

Contexts are crucial in Nginx configuration. The primary contexts used in Nginx are `http`, `server`, and `location`, each serving a different scope within the configuration. Directives placed in the `http` block apply to the entire server. Directives within a `server` block apply to specific virtual servers (defined by server names or port numbers), and those within a `location` block apply only to requests matching a specific location.

40

Variable usage in Nginx configuration offers dynamic configuration capabilities. Variables are denoted with the $ sign, for example, $request_uri. These can be used within directives to define dynamic behaviors based on request parameters.

```
1  server {
2      listen 80;
3      server_name example.com;
4
5      location / {
6          root /var/www/html;
7          try_files $uri $uri/ /index.html;
8      }
9  }
```

Configuring Nginx involves not just placing directives and blocks in a file, but understanding how these configurations interact with each other and with incoming requests. Each directive, block, and context plays a role in how Nginx parses requests and delivers responses, creating a flexible and powerful tool for web serving and reverse proxying.

Comments can be added to Nginx configuration files using the # symbol. Comments are ignored by Nginx and can be used to explain the purpose of specific directives or to temporarily disable them.

```
1  # Listen on port 80
2  listen 80;
```

To successfully apply changes made to the configuration files, Nginx must be reloaded or restarted. This ensures the new settings are read and applied without interrupting ongoing connections. Reloading is done using the nginx -s reload command in the terminal.

Understanding the basic Nginx configuration syntax and structure is the foundation for more advanced server management tasks, such as security enhancements, performance tuning, and handling dynamic content. This foundational knowledge enables administrators to tailor Nginx's behavior to meet the specific needs of their applications and infrastructure.

2.6 Configuring Nginx as a Web Server

Configuring Nginx as a web server is a fundamental task for harnessing its full potential to serve both static and dynamic content to clients over the Internet. This process involves editing the Nginx configuration files, which are, by default, located in the /etc/nginx directory on most Linux distributions. The primary configuration file is named nginx.conf and serves as the entry point for configuring various aspects of Nginx behavior.

To begin the configuration, it's imperative to understand the basic structure of the Nginx configuration file, which is divided into directives and blocks. Directives are name-value pairs separated by spaces and ending with a semicolon (;), while blocks are groups of directives enclosed in braces ({}). A typical Nginx configuration file consists of several context levels, including the events, http, server, and location contexts.

```
 1  http {
 2      server {
 3          listen 80;
 4          server_name example.com www.example.com;
 5
 6          location / {
 7              root /var/www/html;
 8              index index.html index.htm;
 9          }
10
11          location /images/ {
12              root /var/www/html;
13          }
14      }
15  }
```

The above example showcases a basic configuration for serving static content. The server block defines a virtual server listening on port 80. The server_name directive specifies the domain names that this server block will respond to. Inside the server block, the location blocks specify how to handle different URIs. The first location block is set to catch the root URI (/) and serve content from the directory specified in the root directive. The index directive defines which files should be used as the index.

For serving dynamic content, such as content that is processed by

PHP, it's necessary to configure Nginx to pass requests to a backend server or processor. This usually involves setting up a location block with a `proxy_pass` or `fastcgi_pass` directive, depending on the backend being used.

```
1  location ~ \.php$ {
2      fastcgi_pass unix:/var/run/php/php7.4-fpm.sock;
3      fastcgi_index index.php;
4      include fastcgi_params;
5      fastcgi_param SCRIPT_FILENAME $document_root$fastcgi_script_name;
6  }
```

In the example above, requests for URIs ending in .php are processed by a FastCGI server running PHP. The `fastcgi_pass` directive tells Nginx to forward these requests to the specified Unix socket. The `fastcgi_param` directive is used to pass additional parameters to the FastCGI server.

Optimization is another crucial aspect of configuring Nginx for web serving. Performance can be enhanced by adjusting various settings, like buffer sizes, timeouts, and compression. An important directive to consider is the `keepalive_timeout`, which defines how long a connection should stay open for additional requests.

```
1  http {
2      keepalive_timeout 65;
3  }
```

To ensure that Nginx has been correctly configured, testing the configuration file for syntax errors is essential. This can be done by executing the `nginx -t` command. If the test passes, the configuration can be applied by reloading Nginx using `systemctl reload nginx` on systemd-based systems or `service nginx reload` on SysVinit systems.

```
nginx: configuration file /etc/nginx/nginx.conf test is successful
```

Configuring Nginx as a web server involves detailed adjustments to its configuration files to accurately serve static and dynamic content based on incoming requests. Understanding the structure and syntax of these configuration files is paramount to successfully leveraging Nginx's capabilities. With a proper configuration in place, Nginx can

efficiently handle web traffic, serving content quickly and reliably to
end-users.

2.7   Testing and Reloading Nginx Configuration

After modifying Nginx's configuration files, it is crucial to test the
changes for errors before applying them. A syntax or configuration
mistake can render the web server non-functional, adversely affecting the served sites. Nginx provides a simple yet powerful tool for
testing configuration files without disrupting the current service if
the configuration is already running.

To test the configuration files for syntax correctness and basic oper-
ability, use the following command in the terminal:

```
1   sudo nginx -t
```

This command checks all configuration files for syntax errors and
prints the result.   If any errors are found, the command also
specifies the file and line number where the problem occurs,
significantly   simplifying   troubleshooting.   A   successful
configuration test output looks like this:

```
nginx: the configuration file /etc/nginx/nginx.conf syntax is ok
nginx: configuration file /etc/nginx/nginx.conf test is successful
```

In case the changes are confirmed to be error-free, the next step is to
apply them without needing to restart the Nginx service fully. This
is crucial for maintaining the availability of the website or application the server is hosting. Instead of a complete restart, Nginx allows
for a configuration reload, which reads and applies the new configuration without dropping existing connections. To reload the Nginx
configuration, run:

```
1   sudo systemctl reload nginx
```

Alternatively, if not using systemctl, the following command can be
used:

```
1   sudo nginx -s reload
```

Both commands achieve the same effect, but the first relies on the system's service manager while the second is a direct Nginx command.

Reloading the configuration is a smoother process that ensures that new connections use the updated settings, while existing connections continue without interruption. This capability is particularly vital in a production environment where service continuity is paramount.

Despite the safety net provided by the reload feature, it is best practice to test configuration changes during maintenance windows or periods of low traffic. Additionally, maintaining version control or backups of configuration files before making changes is advisable. This approach allows for quick rollbacks if the post-reload behavior is not as expected or if performance issues arise.

In summary, the process of testing and reloading Nginx configurations comprises a critical part of managing a Nginx server. Ensuring configurations are error-free before applying them helps maintain the integrity and availability of services hosted by Nginx. The simple but powerful command-line tools provided by Nginx facilitate a smooth, error-proof workflow for administrators, streamlining the deployment of configuration changes.

2.8   Setting Up Virtual Hosts in Nginx

Setting up virtual hosts, also known as server blocks in Nginx, enables the server to host multiple domains or websites on a single machine. This feature is particularly useful for managing more than one website, each with its own domain name, on the same server. In this section, we will discuss the steps required to configure virtual hosts in Nginx.

The configuration file for Nginx is typically found at /etc/nginx/nginx.conf, with additional server block (virtual host) definitions located in the /etc/nginx/sites-available directory. To enable a site, a symbolic link is created in the

/etc/nginx/sites-enabled directory pointing to its configuration file in the /sites-available directory. This setup allows for easy enabling and disabling of sites.

The basic steps to set up a virtual host (server block) in Nginx are as follows:

- Create a new configuration file for the website in the /etc/nginx/sites-available directory.

- Define the server block within this file, specifying the server name (domain), document root (location of the website files), and any additional settings required.

- Create a symbolic link to this file in the /etc/nginx/sites-enabled directory to enable the site.

- Test the Nginx configuration for syntax errors.

- Reload Nginx to apply changes.

An example of a server block configuration may look like the following:

```
1  server {
2      listen 80;
3      server_name example.com www.example.com;
4
5      location / {
6          root /var/www/example.com;
7          index index.html index.htm;
8      }
9  }
```

This example illustrates a basic server block listening on port 80 for requests to example.com or www.example.com. When requests are received, it serves files from the /var/www/example.com directory, with index.html or index.htm as the default documents to serve.

After creating or modifying a server block file, use the following command to test the Nginx configuration for errors:

```
sudo nginx -t
```

If the configuration test is successful, reload Nginx to apply the changes:

```
sudo systemctl reload nginx
```

Reloading Nginx allows the application to apply configuration changes without dropping existing connections, providing a seamless transition for live environments.

Configuring virtual hosts correctly is central to leveraging the flexibility and power of Nginx in serving multiple websites. This setup not only simplifies management by centralizing configurations but also optimizes resource utilization by consolidating server duties. Properly configured virtual hosts enhance the server's ability to handle diverse web traffic efficiently and securely.

2.9   Enabling HTTPS with SSL/TLS

Enabling HTTPS in Nginx requires the use of SSL (Secure Socket Layer) or its successor, TLS (Transport Layer Security), to encrypt data transmitted between the web server and clients. This encryption ensures that any data, including sensitive or personal information, is securely transmitted over the internet, preventing unauthorized access or interception.

The first step in setting up HTTPS is to obtain a TLS/SSL certificate. This can be done in two primary ways: obtaining a free certificate from Let's Encrypt, a popular certificate authority that provides free certificates aiming to encourage a more secure internet; or purchasing a certificate from a trusted certificate authority.

To obtain a certificate from Let's Encrypt, users can use certbot, an automated tool that simplifies the process of obtaining and renewing certificates. The installation and usage of certbot differ slightly depending on the operating system, but generally involves the following steps:

```
1   sudo apt-get update
```

```
2  sudo apt-get install software-properties-common
3  sudo add-apt-repository universe
4  sudo add-apt-repository ppa:certbot/certbot
5  sudo apt-get update
6  sudo apt-get install certbot python-certbot-nginx
7  sudo certbot --nginx
```

For those opting to purchase a certificate from a certificate authority, the process involves generating a CSR (Certificate Signing Request) and sending it to the authority. Once the CSR is generated and sent, the authority will validate the domain and issue a certificate. The process of generating a CSR in Nginx typically involves the following commands:

```
1  openssl req -new -newkey rsa:2048 -nodes -keyout your_domain_name.key -out
      your_domain_name.csr
```

After obtaining the SSL/TLS certificate, the next step is to configure Nginx to use the certificate for HTTPS. This involves editing the Nginx configuration file for your website, typically found at /etc/nginx/sites-available/your_domain_name.   Add   the following lines inside the server block:

```
1  listen 443 ssl;
2  ssl_certificate /etc/letsencrypt/live/your_domain_name/fullchain.pem;
3  ssl_certificate_key /etc/letsencrypt/live/your_domain_name/privkey.pem;
```

These lines inform Nginx to listen on port 443, the standard port for HTTPS traffic, and specify the locations of the SSL certificate and private key files.

Additionally, it's a best practice to redirect all HTTP traffic to HTTPS to ensure that users are always using a secure connection. This can be accomplished by adding the following server block in the Nginx configuration file:

```
1  server {
2     listen 80;
3     server_name your_domain_name www.your_domain_name;
4     return 301 https://$server_name$request_uri;
5  }
```

This configuration listens for HTTP traffic on port 80 and redirects requests to HTTPS by issuing an HTTP 301 redirect.

Finally, after making the necessary changes to the Nginx configuration files, test the configuration for errors with:

```
1   sudo nginx -t
```

If the test returns "syntax is ok" and "test is successful", proceed to reload Nginx to apply the changes:

```
1   sudo systemctl reload nginx
```

```
Output example:
* Reloading nginx nginx
```

By following these steps, HTTPS has been successfully enabled on your Nginx server, enhancing the security of your web server by encrypting all data in transit.

2.10 Directory Structure and Configuration Files

Understanding the directory structure and configuration files is crucial for efficiently managing and tuning Nginx to meet specific requirements. Nginx, by design, follows a modular structure that segregates its main configuration file from additional settings, server blocks, and module-specific configurations. This design facilitates easier management and customization of server behavior without the risk of disrupting the core configuration.

Main Directory Structure

The primary directory to familiarize oneself with is the Nginx root directory, which varies depending on the installation method and the operating system. Inside this root directory, several subdirectories play pivotal roles in Nginx's functionality:

- /etc/nginx: This is the central directory for Nginx configura-

tions on most Linux distributions. It houses the main configuration file, nginx.conf, and other pertinent directories.

- /etc/nginx/nginx.conf: The main configuration file for
  Nginx that controls global settings, including user
  permissions,   worker   processes,   and   load-balancing
  configurations.

- /etc/nginx/sites-available: This directory is typically
  used to store server block configurations for different
  websites. These configurations are not automatically enabled.

- /etc/nginx/sites-enabled: It contains symbolic links to
  configurations in sites-available that you wish to be
  actively read by Nginx upon startup. The separation between
  sites-available   and   sites-enabled   allows   for
  straightforward enabling and disabling of server blocks.

- /var/log/nginx: Default location for Nginx log files, including
  access logs and error logs. These logs are vital for troubleshooting and optimizing Nginx performance.

- /usr/share/nginx/html: The default directory from which
  Nginx serves static content. This location can be adjusted as
  needed within individual server block configurations.

- /etc/nginx/modules-enabled: Contains configurations for
  dynamically loaded modules, facilitating the extension of
  Nginx functionalities without altering the core binary.

Configuration Files Explained

The nginx.conf file, located within the /etc/nginx directory, is
structured using simple, straightforward syntax that allows for both
simple and complex configurations.   This file is composed of
directives grouped into contexts (also known as blocks), which
define specific behavior for Nginx.

A basic structure of the nginx.conf file is outlined as follows:

```
1   user www-data;
2   worker_processes auto;
3   pid /run/nginx.pid;
4
5   events {
6       worker_connections 1024;
7   }
8
9   http {
10      include /etc/nginx/mime.types;
11      default_type application/octet-stream;
12
13      log_format main '$remote_addr - $remote_user [$time_local] "$request" '
14                      '$status $body_bytes_sent "$http_referer" '
15                      '"$http_user_agent" "$http_x_forwarded_for"';
16
17      access_log /var/log/nginx/access.log main;
18
19      sendfile on;
20      tcp_nopush on;
21      tcp_nodelay on;
22
23      keepalive_timeout 65;
24
25      include /etc/nginx/conf.d/*.conf;
26      include /etc/nginx/sites-enabled/*;
27  }
```

This exemplary configuration initiates basic Nginx functionality including handling of client requests, logging, and serving static content. Notice the inclusion directives at the end of the `http` block, which tell Nginx to incorporate additional configuration files found in the specified directories. This modular approach enables administrators to manage server blocks and specific settings in isolated files, thus maintaining a clean and organized main configuration file.

In addition to the `nginx.conf` file, administrators will often interact with:

- `mime.types`: Defines mappings between file extensions and MIME types, instructing Nginx on how to handle different types of content.

- Server block files in `/etc/nginx/sites-available`: These files define server-specific configurations, such as server names, SSL settings, and locations for handling different URL patterns.

51

By understanding the directory structure and configuration file layout, system administrators and web developers can effectively navigate, manage, and customize Nginx to suit a wide range of hosting scenarios.

2.11   Troubleshooting Common Installation Issues

Troubleshooting is an inevitable part of working with any software, and Nginx is no exception.   The installation process, although straightforward, can occasionally meet with issues. This section will cover common problems that users might encounter during the installation of Nginx and provide detailed solutions to resolve these issues effectively.

Issue 1: Failed to Start Nginx Service

This issue is frequently encountered when attempting to start the Nginx service after installation. The cause can vary, from incorrect configuration files to port conflicts.

- **Solution 1: Check for Syntax Errors in Configuration Files**
  The first step is to ensure there are no syntax errors in your Nginx configuration files. Nginx will not start if it encounters an error. You can check for syntax errors using the command:

```
1    nginx -t
```

  If the output indicates an error, correct it by editing the configuration file in question.

- **Solution 2: Ensure Port Availability**
  Nginx defaults to listening on port 80 for HTTP and port 443 for HTTPS. If another service is already using these ports, Nginx will fail to start. Use the following command to identify if the ports are in use:

```
1    sudo lsof -i :80 -i :443
```

If another service is using these ports, either stop the service or configure Nginx to listen on different ports.

Issue 2: Nginx Fails to Serve Content

After installation and starting the Nginx service, you might find that Nginx is not serving your content as expected. Often, this issue is related to incorrect configuration or permissions errors.

- **Solution 1: Verify Configuration Files**
  Ensure that your server block within /etc/nginx/nginx.conf or the respective site configuration files in /etc/nginx/sites-available/ correctly points to the root directory where your content is located. The root directive should look something like this:

```
1    root /var/www/html;
```

- **Solution 2: Check File Permissions**
  Nginx needs read access to the files and execute access to the directories it serves. If Nginx is unable to access these files due to permission issues, it will not serve them. Ensure that the permissions are set correctly:

```
1    sudo chmod -R 755 /var/www/html
```

This command sets the read and execute permissions for the user, group, and others on the /var/www/html directory.

Issue 3: SSL/TLS Handshake Failure

A common issue when setting up HTTPS is that the SSL/TLS handshake may fail. This failure can happen for various reasons, including mismatched certificates, outdated cipher suites, or incorrect server block configuration.

53

- **Solution 1: Verify Certificate and Key Files**
  Check that the SSL certificate and key files specified in your Nginx configuration match and are correctly formatted. The directives for specifying these files in your server block should look similar to:

```
1  ssl_certificate /etc/ssl/certs/nginx.crt;
2  ssl_certificate_key /etc/ssl/private/nginx.key;
```

- **Solution 2: Update Cipher Suites**
  Ensure that you are using modern, secure cipher suites in your Nginx configuration. You can specify the suites with the following directive:

```
1  ssl_ciphers 'ECDHE-ECDSA-AES128-GCM-SHA256:ECDHE-RSA-AES128-GCM-SHA256:
      ECDHE-ECDSA-AES256-GCM-SHA384:ECDHE-RSA-AES256-GCM-SHA384:DHE-RSA
      -AES128-GCM-SHA256:DHE-RSA-AES256-GCM-SHA384';
```

Resolving common installation issues requires an understanding of the underlying problem and applying the appropriate solution. By following the troubleshooting steps outlined above, you can mitigate most problems encountered during the Nginx installation process.

2.12 Upgrading and Uninstalling Nginx

Upgrading or uninstalling Nginx necessitates a clear understanding of the installation process and the system's package management. This section will explain how to efficiently perform these operations across different operating systems, ensuring minimal disruption to service.

Upgrading Nginx: Upgrading Nginx can be critical for accessing new features, security patches, and performance improvements. The upgrading process varies between operating systems, but commonly involves package management systems like apt for Debian-based systems, yum for RHEL-based systems, and Homebrew for macOS.

- For Debian-based systems, initiate the upgrade by updating

the package lists using sudo apt-get update. Once the
package lists are updated, perform the upgrade by executing
sudo apt-get install nginx.

- On RHEL-based systems, the process begins with sudo yum
makecache to refresh the package cache. Following this, sudo
yum install nginx will perform the upgrade.

- macOS users leveraging Homebrew can upgrade Nginx by
running brew update followed by brew upgrade nginx.

It's recommended to back up configuration files before proceeding
with an upgrade. This precaution ensures that custom configurations
are not lost. After upgrading, it's crucial to test the configuration
using the nginx -t command, which checks for any syntax errors or
misconfigurations.

Uninstalling Nginx: Removing Nginx from a system is straightforward but requires caution to ensure that all components, including
configuration files and logs, are adequately addressed.

- To uninstall Nginx on Debian-based systems, use the
command sudo apt-get purge nginx nginx-common. The
purge option is employed to remove both the package and its
configuration files.

- On RHEL-based systems, execute sudo yum remove nginx.
Following this, manually check for remaining configuration
files and logs, which might need to be removed using rm.

- For macOS users with Nginx installed via Homebrew, brew
uninstall nginx will remove the application. Additional
checks should be made for any leftover configuration or log
files in /usr/local/etc/nginx or /var/log/nginx,
respectively.

Prior to uninstallation, review and back up any necessary configuration files or logs for future reference. This practice ensures that valuable data is not inadvertently lost.

After uninstalling, it might be necessary to halt any system services or processes that depended on Nginx. Confirm the complete removal by checking if the Nginx service is deactivated and no longer present in the system's process list.

This section has elucidated the detailed procedures to upgrade and uninstall Nginx across multiple operating systems, prioritizing safety and integrity of the system configurations and data.

Chapter 3

Understanding Nginx Architecture and Processing Phases

The architecture of Nginx is designed for high concurrency, performance, and efficient use of resources, featuring an event-driven, asynchronous approach. Understanding this architecture is crucial for effectively configuring and optimizing Nginx's performance. The processing phases of Nginx, from client request handling to response delivery, involve a sequence of operations executed in a well-defined order. This includes the processing of static and dynamic content, the application of various modules, and the handling of connections. Insights into these phases and the architecture as a whole provide a solid foundation for mastering Nginx's capabilities and extending its functionality.

3.1 Overview of Nginx Architecture

Nginx, pronounced as "Engine-X", stands distinguished amongst web servers for its high concurrency, performance, and efficient resource usage. At its core, Nginx employs an event-driven, asynchronous architecture. This architecture is fundamentally designed to handle a massive number of connections simultaneously. Unlike traditional server processes that spawn new processes or threads for each request, Nginx operates on a non-blocking, event-driven model. This section unfolds the layers of Nginx's architecture to offer a comprehensive understanding essential for leveraging its prowess.

The cornerstone of Nginx's architecture is its master-worker process model. When the Nginx service is initiated, it launches a single master process and multiple worker processes. The master process's role is to read and validate configuration files, manage worker processes, and handle administrative tasks without partaking in client request processing. In contrast, worker processes, spawned by the master process, are the workhorses of Nginx. They handle network connections, process client requests, and execute request handling phases.

- The master process is launched upon starting the Nginx service.

- Worker processes are spawned by the master process to handle client requests.

The architecture's event-driven nature is facilitated by an efficient mechanism that allows a worker process to handle thousands of connections. These connections are managed through a non-blocking I/O mechanism. Specifically, when a request is received, it is immediately attached to an event. As events occur (e.g., a request is fully received, data is ready to be sent), the corresponding connections are activated for processing without blocking other operations. This model contrasts sharply with the thread-per-connection approach, significantly reducing memory overhead and increasing scalability.

```
Master Process -> Reads and validates configuration
Worker Process -> Handles requests
```

Nginx's architecture is modular, comprised of core modules and third-party modules that can be dynamically loaded or compiled at installation. These modules extend the functionality of Nginx, allowing it to process a wide range of requests, including static file serving, proxying to backend servers, and executing server-side code through gateway interfaces.

Equipped with an understanding of Nginx's architecture, including its master-worker model, event-driven processing, and modular design, one can better appreciate the server's ability to efficiently manage resources and handle a high volume of concurrent connections. This foundation is crucial for delving deeper into the intricacies of Nginx's request processing, configuration, and optimization strategies discussed in subsequent sections.

3.2   Event-Driven Model Explained

Nginx adopts an event-driven model to efficiently manage connections and requests. This model stands in contrast to the traditional thread-per-connection handling strategy, allowing Nginx to support thousands of concurrent connections with a minimal footprint on system resources. The event-driven approach leverages asynchronous, non-blocking I/O operations, eliminating the need for multiple threads or processes to handle simultaneous connections. This section breaks down the components and workings of this model, providing insight into its efficiency and performance advantages.

The core of the event-driven model revolves around events and event handlers. An event can be any significant occurrence, such as the receipt of a new connection, receipt of data, or a timeout. Each event is associated with an event handler, a function that is triggered when its corresponding event occurs. Nginx efficiently manages these events using a mechanism known as an event loop.

```
1   // Pseudo code example of an event loop
2   while (events_exist) {
3       event = get_next_event();
4       handle_event(event);
5   }
```

In the context of Nginx, the event loop repeatedly checks for new events (such as incoming connections or data from clients), and dispatches these events to their respective handlers. The efficiency of this model is largely due to its non-blocking nature. When an I/O operation (like reading from a network socket) is initiated, Nginx does not wait for the operation to complete; instead, it continues to process other tasks. Once the I/O operation completes, an event is generated and handled accordingly.

Nginx employs specific mechanisms to detect and dispatch events efficiently, known as event notification mechanisms. These mechanisms, which include epoll (on Linux), kqueue (on BSD systems), and select, are crucial for monitoring multiple connections simultaneously for any signs of activity. The use of an efficient event notification mechanism allows Nginx to quickly identify active connections from the thousands that it may be monitoring, without significant resource consumption.

- epoll is highly scalable and generally the preferred method on Linux systems.

- kqueue is used on BSD systems and offers similar scalability and performance.

- select, although widely supported, is less efficient and generally used as a fallback.

The event-driven model enables Nginx to manage a high volume of connections simultaneously with high efficiency and low latency. This model is particularly well-suited to handling HTTP requests, which are inherently asynchronous. Clients initiate requests without a predetermined order, and responses are sent as soon as the requested data is available, without blocking other operations. This asynchronous handling ensures that resources are used efficiently, and performance is maximized, making Nginx an excellent choice for high-traffic websites and applications.

To better illustrate the advantages of Nginx's event-driven model, consider the alternative: a thread-per-connection model. In this model, each connection requires a dedicated thread or process. Managing thousands of threads can quickly overwhelm system resources, leading to degraded performance and scalability issues. By contrast, Nginx's event-driven, asynchronous model avoids these pitfalls, offering superior scalability and resource efficiency.

In summary, the event-driven model is a cornerstone of Nginx's architecture, enabling it to handle numerous concurrent connections efficiently. This model is characterized by its use of events, event handlers, and an event loop, coupled with efficient event notification mechanisms. This approach minimizes resource consumption and maximizes performance, making Nginx well-suited for environments where high concurrency and efficiency are required.

3.3 Worker Processes and Their Roles

Nginx utilizes a master-worker architecture to efficiently manage connections and requests. In this architecture, there is a single master process and multiple worker processes. The master process is responsible for managing the worker processes, including reading and validating configuration files, creating worker processes, and handling administrative tasks like graceful shutdowns and restarts. Worker processes handle the actual processing of client requests. This section delves into the functionality and significance of worker processes within Nginx's operation.

When Nginx starts, the master process parses the configuration files and, based on their directives, spawns a predetermined number of worker processes. The number of worker processes is configurable, allowing for scalability and adaptability to various hardware capabilities and workloads. A common configuration is to set the number of worker processes equal to the number of CPU cores available, maximizing the utilization of hardware resources.

Each worker process in Nginx operates independently, running in a non-blocking, event-driven loop to handle multiple connections simultaneously. Their operation is based on the epoll (Linux), kqueue (BSD-based systems), or select mechanism, depending on the underlying operating system. This approach allows Nginx to achieve high concurrency and performance, managing thousands of connections per worker process with minimal memory overhead.

Worker Process Configuration Example:

```
1  http {
2      worker_processes 4; # Configures Nginx to use 4 worker processes
3      events {
4          worker_connections 1024; # Each worker process can handle 1024 connections
5      }
6  }
```

The distribution of client connections among worker processes is managed by the operating system's kernel. Using mechanisms like epoll or kqueue, the system efficiently distributes incoming connections to available worker processes, ensuring a balanced workload and minimizing context switching and process locking overhead.

One of the pivotal roles of worker processes is to execute various phases of request processing, from parsing the HTTP request to communicating with upstream servers and forming the HTTP response. Worker processes evaluate the configuration directives specified in the Nginx configuration files, determining how to process each request. This includes handling static content directly, interfacing with the PSGI/WSGI applications, or reverse proxying requests to other servers.

Beyond their primary role in request processing, worker processes also perform other critical functions, such as:

- **Access control and request filtering**, wherein worker processes evaluate client request headers and other parameters against configured rules, allowing or denying access accordingly.

- **Request and response transformation**, which may involve modifying headers, content rewriting, or compression before sending responses to clients.

- **Logging and monitoring**, where worker processes record request and error logs, providing valuable insights for debugging, performance optimization, and monitoring.

- **SSL/TLS handshake and encryption**, in cases where Nginx is configured to serve HTTPS traffic, worker processes manage the secure socket layer handshake and encryption processes.

Effective configuration and tuning of worker processes are crucial for optimizing Nginx's performance and resource utilization. Factors like hardware specifications, the nature of the workload (CPU-intensive, IO-bound, or mixed), and the expected traffic volume influence the optimal configuration. Regular monitoring and performance analysis can guide adjustments to the number of worker processes and connections, ensuring that Nginx operates efficiently under varying conditions.

Worker processes are the backbone of Nginx's high-performance, event-driven architecture. Their independent, asynchronous operation allows Nginx to handle numerous client requests concurrently, making it a robust solution for high-traffic web servers, reverse proxies, and load balancers. Understanding the roles and optimal configuration of worker processes is essential for leveraging the full power of Nginx.

3.4 Handling Client Requests

In this section, we explore how Nginx processes incoming client requests. A request sent by a client first reaches an Nginx server listening on a specified port. Upon arrival, Nginx categorizes the request into either a static or dynamic request. The differentiation between these two types of requests is paramount because it determines the subsequent handling path within Nginx's architecture.

Static Content Processing

When a request for static content is received, Nginx bypasses the need for generating content dynamically, instead serving it directly from the disk. This process is significantly faster due to the reduced computation and absence of back-end interaction. For serving static content, Nginx employs an efficient mechanism that involves the following steps:

- Reading the requested file path from the client's HTTP request.

- Searching for the file in the defined location blocks, adhering to the matching criteria specified in the server configuration.

- Retrieving the file from the disk, if it exists and the client has the necessary permissions to access it.

- Sending the file back to the client as an HTTP response.

Dynamic Content Processing

Dynamic content generation involves more complex handling. When a request for dynamic content is identified, Nginx acts as a reverse proxy, forwarding the request to an appropriate back-end handler like PHP-FPM for PHP, or using the uwsgi protocol for Python applications. This process includes:

- Parsing the client's request to determine its nature and intended destination.

- Selecting the appropriate back-end service based on the server configuration.

- Proxying the request to the chosen back-end service.

- Waiting for the back-end service to process the request and generate the response.

- Receiving the generated response from the back-end service.

- Forwarding the response to the client.

Connection Handling

The handling of client requests by Nginx is underpinned by its event-driven model, allowing it to manage multiple connections concurrently within a single worker process. This capability is critical for achieving high performance and scalability. The following outline describes the connection handling procedure:

- A client establishes a connection to the Nginx server.

- Nginx accepts the connection and processes it asynchronously.

- The connection is then added to an event loop, where it's monitored for events such as read or write operations.

- When a request is fully read, Nginx processes it according to the configuration (static or dynamic content serving).

- Upon generating the response, either from disk (static content) or from a back-end service (dynamic content), Nginx writes the response back to the client.

- The connection can be kept alive for further requests or closed based on the client's request headers and server configuration.

Understanding the intricacies of how Nginx handles client requests, differentiates between static and dynamic content, and manages connections effectively is fundamental for optimizing performance and resource usage. This knowledge also serves as a basis for further exploration of Nginx's capabilities, including configuration of server blocks and contexts, optimization techniques, and advanced functionality provided by various Nginx modules.

3.5   The Phases of Request Processing

The request processing pipeline of Nginx is pivotal in understanding how it efficiently manages and serves content. This pipeline is composed of several phases, each dedicated to a specific aspect of the request handling process. Let's delve into the notable phases of Nginx request processing, providing an insight into how requests are handled and how responses are generated and delivered.

Post-Read Phase: This is the initial phase wherein Nginx starts processing a client's request. Modules activated during this phase have the opportunity to modify the request or make early decisions about the request processing flow. This phase can be instrumental for tasks such as request logging or initial access checks.

```
1  location / {
2      client_body_timeout 10s;
3      ...
4  }
```

Server Rewrite Phase: Following the post-read phase, if the request needs to be rewritten or redirected, it is handled in this phase. This involves modifying the request URI according to specific rules defined in the Nginx configuration. The server rewrite phase applies to the server context.

```
1  rewrite ^/oldpath$ /newpath permanent;
```

Location Phase: After the server rewrite phase, Nginx selects the most appropriate location block to handle the request. The selection is based on the location directives defined in the Nginx configuration. This phase is crucial because it determines how the request will be processed further, depending on the matching location block.

```
1  location /images/ {
2      root /data;
3  }
```

Location Rewrite Phase: Similar to the server rewrite phase, this phase allows for the rewriting of the request URI but is applied within the context of the selected location block. Rules defined in this phase can alter the request's processing logic after the location has been selected.

```
1  location /user/ {
2      rewrite ^/user/(.*)$ /show_user.php?user=$1 last;
3  }
```

Access Phase: The access phase is where Nginx performs access control checks to determine if the request should proceed. Access rules can be based on various criteria, including IP addresses, request methods, or user credentials.

```
1  location /admin/ {
2      allow 192.168.1.0/24;
3      deny all;
4  }
```

Content Generation Phase: This is the core phase where Nginx decides how to fulfill the client's request. The decision might involve serving static content directly from the filesystem, passing the request to a reverse proxy, or executing the request through FastCGI or similar mechanisms for dynamic content.

```
1  location / {
2      root /var/www/html;
3      index index.html index.htm;
4  }
```

Log Phase: Finally, after the response is generated and sent to the client, Nginx logs the request as specified by the log directives in the Nginx configuration. This phase is critical for monitoring and debugging.

```
1  access_log /var/log/nginx/access.log;
2  error_log /var/log/nginx/error.log;
```

The phases described above illustrate a simplified overview of the request processing in Nginx. By understanding these phases, administrators and developers can better configure Nginx, ensuring optimized handling of requests that best suits their application's architecture and intended user experience.

3.6 Understanding Server Blocks and Contexts

Nginx utilizes a flexible and extensive configuration system that is principally anchored on the concepts of server blocks and contexts.

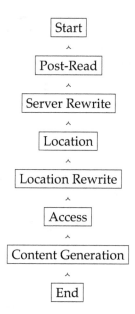

Figure 3.1: Sequence of Nginx request processing phases

These constructs are pivotal for orchestrating how incoming requests are mapped to various resources and processed.

Server blocks are, in essence, the Nginx equivalent to virtual hosts in Apache. They enable the server to distinguish between requests intended for different domain names, IP addresses, or ports and serve the content accordingly. The server block is delineated by braces {}, and within it, directives are specified that configure how requests matching the server block criteria are handled.

```
1   server {
2       listen 80;
3       server_name example.com www.example.com;
4       root /var/www/example;
5       index index.html index.htm;
6   }
```

In the above code snippet, the server is instructed to listen on port 80 for incoming HTTP requests. The server_name directive specifies that this server block will respond to requests for example.com and www.example.com. The document root, where the files to be served are located, is set using the root directive, and the index directive tells Nginx which files to consider as index files.

Contexts in Nginx facilitate the grouping of directives into logical units, affecting their scope and inheritance. The context types include but are not limited to http, server, location, and if contexts, each serving a specific purpose and influencing the application's behavior at different stages of the request processing pipeline. Directives defined in a particular context apply to that context and, in some cases, to nested contexts, enabling precise control over the configuration.

For instance, the http context is used for directives that apply to all server blocks (unless overridden within a server block), while directives within a server context apply only to the particular server block.

```
1   http {
2       index index.html;
3
4       server {
5           listen 80;
6           server_name www.example.com;
```

```
7
8      location / {
9          root /var/www/example;
10     }
11
12     location /images/ {
13         root /var/www/example/images;
14     }
15   }
16 }
```

In the configuration above, the index directive is placed within the http context, setting the index file for all server blocks defined within the http context. Within the server block, there are two location contexts defined, each specifying the root for different URL paths.

Understanding the nuances of server blocks and contexts is paramount for leveraging Nginx's flexibility and power. Correctly configuring these allows for the efficient serving of static content, the reverse proxying of dynamic content, and the application of security policies and redirections with precision.

3.7 Location Blocks: Matching and Processing

Location blocks in Nginx configuration files are vital in determining how requests to specific URIs are handled. They define the processing behavior for requests based on the request URI. Understanding how these blocks match requests and how they are processed is essential for configuring Nginx to serve resources efficiently and securely.

Matching Syntax

Nginx uses location blocks within server blocks to inspect the incoming request's URI and decides which configuration should be applied based on the match. The basic syntax of a location block is:

```
1  location [modifier] /uri/ {
2      ...
```

```
3 | }
```

Modifiers control the matching behavior. Absence of a modifier implies a prefix match. The available modifiers are:

- = for an exact match.

- ~ for a case-sensitive regular expression match.

- ~* for a case-insensitive regular expression match.

- ^~ for a preferential prefix match.

- @ for named locations.

Each modifier influences how Nginx selects a location block when multiple blocks could potentially match a request.

Processing Order

Nginx follows a specific order when evaluating location blocks to determine the best match:

1. Exact matches (=) are evaluated first. If an exact match is found, its corresponding configuration is applied immediately, and the search stops.

2. Among the prefixes, the modifier ^~ signifies that if such a location matches, searching stops, and Nginx does not evaluate regular expressions.

3. Regular expressions are evaluated in the order of their appearance in the configuration file. The first regular expression to match the request's URI wins, and its associated block is applied.

4. If no regular expression matches are found, the longest matching prefix location is selected.

Named Locations

Named locations, initiated with the @ symbol, provide a way to redirect or internally route requests to a specific location block based on dynamic conditions processed in other areas of the configuration. A named location is not directly matched with the request's URI but can be used in combination with directives like try_files for advanced request processing scenarios.

Example Configuration

An illustrative example of handling different URIs using various location blocks is shown below:

```
 1  server {
 2      location = / {
 3          # Exact match for the root URI
 4          ...
 5      }
 6
 7      location /images/ {
 8          # Handles all requests under the /images/ URI
 9          ...
10      }
11
12      location ~* \.(gif|jpg|png)$ {
13          # Case-insensitive regular expression match for image file extensions
14          ...
15      }
16
17      location @fallback {
18          # Named location for custom processing
19          ...
20      }
21  }
```

This example demonstrates the use of exact, prefix, regular expression, and named location matches to control request processing.

Variables and Their Scope

Within location blocks, variables can be set and used to modify request processing behavior dynamically. The scope of these variables is limited to the current request's processing context. For instance:

```
1  location /app/ {
2     set $example "value";
3     ...
4  }
```

Here, the variable $example is set to "value" only within the context of requests matching the /app/ location.

In summary, understanding and configuring location blocks effectively is key to optimizing Nginx's request handling. By properly utilizing match modifiers, processing order rules, and named locations, server administrators can finely tune how requests are handled, leading to improved performance, security, and resource management.

3.8 Variables and Their Scope

In the context of Nginx, variables play a pivotal role in dynamically controlling the behavior of various aspects of request processing, including server response, redirection, and configuration complexities. Variables in Nginx are defined with a diverse scope and lifespan, directly influencing their applicability and behavior across different phases of request processing.

Nginx variables are essentially key-value pairs where the key represents the variable name, prefixed with a dollar sign ($), and the value is dynamically assigned during request handling. The scope of a variable in Nginx can be primarily categorized into two types: built-in variables, which are predefined by Nginx and are automatically populated based on the request and response context, and custom variables, which can be defined by users for specific requirements.

Built-in Variables: These variables are inherently available within Nginx and include client request details such as $request_uri and server details like $host. Built-in variables are globally accessible within the server configuration and provide essential information for request processing.

Custom Variables: Custom variables extend Nginx's flexibility by allowing users to define their own variables using the set directive within the server, location, or if contexts. A custom variable is declared as follows:

```
set $variable_name 'value';
```

It is imperative to understand that the scope of a custom variable is limited to the context in which it is defined. For instance, a variable defined in a server block is accessible within that server block and its child blocks, including location blocks.

Scope and Visibility: The visibility of variables in Nginx is determined by the context in which they are defined. Variables defined in the http block are globally accessible, while those defined in server or location blocks are confined to their respective scopes. Moreover, variable scope can be influenced by directives such as include or server_name.

In addition, the lifecycle of a variable in Nginx, which refers to the duration for which the variable retains its value, is crucial for effectively utilizing variables in dynamic configurations. Custom variables, once set, retain their value within the defined scope until they are overwritten or the request processing completes.

Consider the following example where a custom variable is used to conditionally redirect clients based on a request header:

```
map $http_upgrade $connection_upgrade {
    default upgrade;
    '' close;
}
server {
    ...
    location /websocket {
        proxy_set_header Upgrade $http_upgrade;
        proxy_set_header Connection $connection_upgrade;
        ...
    }
}
```

In this example, the $connection_upgrade variable's value depends on the $http_upgrade header from the client's request. The map block defines a conditional assignment to

$connection_upgrade, demonstrating how variables can be dynamically utilized based on request attributes.

: Understanding the scope and lifecycle of variables in Nginx is vital for crafting efficient, dynamic configurations. Properly leveraging both built-in and custom variables can significantly enhance Nginx's flexibility, allowing it to adapt to diverse web serving scenarios. Mastery of variables empowers administrators to optimize configuration readability and maintainability, thereby facilitating the fine-tuning of server behavior tailored to specific hosting environments.

3.9 Rewrite Rules and Their Execution

Rewrite rules in Nginx serve the pivotal function of allowing the server to modify parts of the request before it completes processing. This capability is particularly useful for redirecting URLs, transforming request arguments, or applying specific configuration directives based on the request's characteristics. Understanding how rewrite rules are executed within Nginx's processing phases is essential for effective server management and optimization of web applications.

Rewrite rules can be defined in either server or location contexts, enabling a high degree of flexibility in how requests are handled. These rules are processed at an early stage in the request lifecycle, directly following the initial request parsing. It is important to note that rewrite directives do not terminate request processing; rather, they alter the request's attributes and then allow processing to continue.

The primary directive used for rewriting in Nginx is rewrite. The rewrite directive follows a basic syntax pattern, which can be described as:

```
1   rewrite regex replacement [flag];
```

Here, regex refers to a regular expression that is matched against the request URI. If a match is found, the URI is transformed into the replacement specified. The optional `flag` parameter can alter the behavior of the rewrite, with common flags being `last`, `break`, `redirect`, and `permanent`.

Let's consider an example where all requests to a specific directory in a domain are to be redirected to a new directory. The corresponding rewrite rule would be as follows:

```
1   rewrite ^/old-directory/(.*)$ /new-directory/$1 permanent;
```

In this example, any request URI that starts with `/old-directory/` will be permanently redirected (HTTP 301 status code) to `/new-directory/` with the rest of the URI preserved and appended.

Nginx processes rewrite directives in a sequential manner, following the order they are defined in the configuration. If multiple `rewrite` directives are present, Nginx will check each one until a directive with the `last` flag is encountered, which signals Nginx to stop processing further rewrite rules and proceed with the next phase of request handling.

Furthermore, Nginx's rewrite module offers additional directives such as `return` and `set`, which can be used in tandem with rewrite rules for more complex request manipulation and redirection scenarios. The `return` directive stops processing and returns a specific status code and text, while the `set` directive allows setting the value of a variable, which can be utilized in rewrite conditions.

```
1   location /example {
2       set $example_variable "some_value";
3       if ($request_uri ~ ^/example/special-case$) {
4           rewrite ^(.*)$ /special-redirect$1 break;
5       }
6       return 200 $example_variable;
7   }
```

In the above example, a variable is set and a conditional rewrite is applied for a specific request URI. If the condition is met, the request is rewritten to `/special-redirect` with the original request URI appended. The `return` directive then outputs a 200 status code and the value of $example_variable.

Understanding and leveraging rewrite rules and their execution is instrumental in tailoring the request processing behavior of Nginx to suit specific requirements. Proper application of these rules helps in efficiently managing redirects, crafting SEO-friendly URLs, and implementing custom request handling logic.

3.10 The Role of SSL/TLS in Request Processing

With the increasing demands for secure transmission of data over the internet, the significance of SSL/TLS in web server configurations, notably in Nginx, has ascended to paramount importance. SSL (Secure Sockets Layer) and TLS (Transport Layer Security) are essential protocols for encrypting communication between web clients and servers, thus ensuring data integrity and confidentiality. In Nginx, the SSL/TLS setup not only promotes security but also influences request processing in several ways.

To comprehend the role of SSL/TLS in Nginx's request processing, it's crucial to break down the SSL/TLS handshake process. This process involves multiple steps where the server and client exchange messages to acknowledge each other's existence, share encryption algorithms, and establish a secure connection before any actual data is exchanged. The configuration of SSL/TLS in Nginx dictates how efficiently these steps are executed, affecting overall server performance and security.

First, consider the initiation of an SSL/TLS handshake:

1. A client requests a secure connection by sending a "ClientHello" message, which includes supported encryption methods, SSL/TLS versions, and other necessary details.

2. Nginx responds with a "ServerHello" message, selecting the encryption method and SSL/TLS version based on the server's configuration and client's capabilities.

During this exchange, Nginx's role is critical. The server must be configured to support a range of encryption methods and SSL/TLS versions to cater to different client capabilities while prioritizing strong encryption algorithms to enhance security. To specify SSL/TLS settings in Nginx, directives are placed within the server block:

```
1  server {
2      listen 443 ssl;
3      ssl_certificate /path/to/ssl_certificate.crt;
4      ssl_certificate_key /path/to/private_key.key;
5      ssl_protocols TLSv1.2 TLSv1.3;
6      ssl_ciphers HIGH:!aNULL:!MD5;
7  }
```

Once the handshake phase is complete, Nginx and the client have established a secure communication channel. All subsequent data exchanged between the client and server, including the HTTP request itself, is encrypted. This phase significantly impacts the latency of the initial request, as SSL/TLS handshake operates additionally to the HTTP request/response cycle.

Regarding the request processing, SSL/TLS affects Nginx in the following ways:

- **Performance** mainly through the SSL/TLS handshake operation. Nginx optimizes this by supporting session caching and session tickets, reducing the handshake overhead for subsequent connections.

- **Configuration Complexity**, as maintaining high security requires a detailed and often updated configuration to use strong ciphers, protocol versions, and SSL/TLS features like OCSP Stapling.

Finally, the secure handling of SSL/TLS in Nginx involves not only server configuration but also vigilant monitoring and updating. This ensures compliance with the latest security standards and practices, allowing Nginx to efficiently process client requests without compromising security.

As SSL/TLS plays a crucial role in client request processing in Nginx, understanding and configuring these protocols correctly enhances security and performance, establishing a reliable and secure environment for web applications.

3.11   Logging and Error Handling

Logging and error handling are pivotal aspects of managing and troubleshooting Nginx servers, offering insights into server activity and potential issues. Nginx segregates its logging into two primary types: access logs and error logs. Each log serves a distinct purpose, enabling administrators to monitor server operations effectively and identify problems promptly.

Access Logs record every request processed by the Nginx server. The default configuration captures essential details such as the client's IP address, request time, method, URI, status code, byte size of the response, and the user agent. Access logs are configurable; administrators can specify which data to log by modifying the log format directive `log_format` within the http, server, or location context. An example of customizing the log format is shown below:

```
1   log_format main '$remote_addr - $remote_user [$time_local] "$request" '
2                   '$status $body_bytes_sent "$http_referer" '
3                   '"$http_user_agent" "$http_x_forwarded_for"';
```

This customization enables the logging of additional information such as the HTTP referer and the X-Forwarded-For header value, which can be crucial for analyzing client behavior or detecting potential security threats.

Error Logs detail the issues encountered by the server, including problems with parsing configuration files, connection errors, and software bugs. Nginx allows for the adjustment of the error log verbosity by setting the log level directive. The available log levels are: debug, info, notice, warn, error, crit, alert, and emerg. The configuration snippet below sets the error log level to `warn`, which captures warnings and more severe messages:

```
1   error_log /var/log/nginx/error.log warn;
```

It is important to note that logging at a very verbose level, such as debug, can generate large amounts of log data, which might affect server performance. Therefore, it's advisable to use more verbose logging levels only when troubleshooting specific issues.

Log Rotation is a crucial practice for managing log files' size and ensuring that logging does not consume excessive disk space. While Nginx does not provide an in-built log rotation feature, most operating systems offer logrotate, a utility which can automatically compress, rotate, remove, and mail log files. A typical logrotate configuration for Nginx might look as follows:

```
/var/log/nginx/*.log {
    daily
    missingok
    rotate 14
    compress
    delaycompress
    notifempty
    create 0640 nginx adm
    sharedscripts
    postrotate
        [ ! -f /var/run/nginx.pid ] || kill -USR1 `cat /var/run/nginx.pid`
    endscript
}
```

This configuration rotates logs daily, keeps fourteen days of logs, compresses the rotated logs, and signals Nginx to reopen log files after rotation with the USR1 signal.

Effective logging and error handling are fundamental for maintaining an optimally functioning Nginx server. Through meticulous configuration of access and error logs, administrators can glean vital information for monitoring server health, understanding client interactions, and troubleshooting problems as they arise. Coupled with responsible log management practices such as log rotation, logging becomes a powerful tool in the Nginx administrator's arsenal.

3.12 Optimizing Resource Usage and Performance

Optimization of resource usage and performance in Nginx entails a series of strategic adjustments and configurations aimed at enhancing the efficiency and speed at which Nginx processes requests and delivers responses. This section delves into various techniques and best practices for achieving optimal performance, including tuning worker processes, using caching mechanisms effectively, configuring buffer sizes, and leveraging Nginx's Gzip compression.

1. Tuning Worker Processes:

Nginx's ability to handle numerous concurrent connections efficiently is largely attributed to its worker process architecture. Each worker process handles a subset of the total client connections, and their number should be congruent with the number of CPU cores for optimal performance. This alignment ensures that each worker can execute on a separate core without unnecessary context switching or contention.

```
1  worker_processes auto;
```

Setting the worker_processes directive to auto allows Nginx to automatically spawn a worker process per CPU core available, optimizing CPU usage.

2. Efficient Use of Caching:

Caching is a critical aspect of performance optimization in Nginx. By storing frequently accessed files in memory, Nginx can serve these files from the cache instead of reading them from disk, significantly reducing I/O operations and response times.

```
1  http {
2      ...
3      proxy_cache_path /data/nginx/cache levels=1:2 keys_zone=my_cache:10m max_size
           =10g
4      inactive=60m use_temp_path=off;
5  }
```

The above configuration defines a cache zone named my_cache, specifying its path, memory size, disk size, and duration of inactivity before an item is considered stale.

3. Configuring Buffer Sizes:

Proper configuration of buffer sizes can help prevent bottleneck situations, where Nginx spends excessive time reading from or writing to client connections. The buffer sizes should be adjusted based on the typical size of the requests and responses handled by your server.

```
1   client_body_buffer_size 128k;
2   client_header_buffer_size 1k;
3   client_max_body_size 10m;
4   large_client_header_buffers 4 4k;
```

These directives adjust the buffer sizes for the client body and headers, ensuring that Nginx can process requests and responses efficiently without having to resort to temporary files.

4. Leveraging Gzip Compression:

Gzip compression reduces the size of the responses before they are sent over the network, lowering the amount of data transmitted and, consequently, the response time. Nginx provides robust support for Gzip compression, which can be enabled and configured as shown below:

```
1   gzip on;
2   gzip_types text/plain application/xml application/json;
3   gzip_min_length 1000;
```

Enabling Gzip and specifying which types of content should be compressed ensures that only responses benefiting from compression are processed, bypassing smaller responses where compression could be counterproductive.

Implementing these optimizations can lead to significant improvements in the resource utilization and performance of Nginx servers. By carefully adjusting settings in line with the specific characteristics and requirements of your workload, Nginx can be tuned to deliver fast, reliable service to clients, even under high load conditions.

Chapter 4

Configuring Web Servers: Domains, SSL, and HTTPS

Configuring Nginx as a web server involves setting up domains, securing connections with SSL/TLS, and enforcing HTTPS to enhance security and privacy. This configuration ensures that web applications are delivered efficiently and securely to end-users. Proper domain configuration aids in the organization and scalability of web services, while SSL/TLS encryption protects data in transit against interception and tampering. The transition to HTTPS not only boosts security but also improves search rankings and user trust. Mastering these configurations in Nginx is essential for maintaining robust, secure, and high-performance web services.

4.1   Domain Name Configuration in Nginx

Configuring domain names in Nginx is a critical first step in setting up a web server that is both efficient and scalable. Domain name configuration allows Nginx to serve different content based on the requested domain, enabling the hosting of multiple websites on a single server. This section delineates the process of configuring domain names in Nginx, from the basic setup to more advanced configurations.

Basic Domain Name Configuration

The basic configuration of a domain in Nginx involves editing the Nginx configuration file, typically found at /etc/nginx/nginx.conf, or more commonly, creating a new file under /etc/nginx/sites-available/ and linking it to /etc/nginx/sites-enabled/. Here is a step-by-step guide to configuring a simple domain:

1. Start by creating a new configuration file for your domain in /etc/nginx/sites-available/. The file name should ideally match your domain name for easy identification. For example, for the domain example.com, you might create example.com.conf.

```
1   sudo touch /etc/nginx/sites-available/example.com.conf
```

2. Edit the newly created configuration file using a text editor of your choice:

```
1   sudo nano /etc/nginx/sites-available/example.com.conf
```

3. Add the following basic configuration directives to the file. Adjust the server_name to your domain name and root to the directory where your website's files are located:

```
1   server {
2       listen 80;
3       server_name example.com www.example.com;
4       root /var/www/example.com;
5
6       location / {
7           try_files $uri $uri/ =404;
8       }
9   }
```

4. Enable the site by creating a symbolic link to the configuration file in /etc/nginx/sites-enabled/:

```
1  sudo ln -s /etc/nginx/sites-available/example.com.conf /etc/nginx/sites-
       enabled/
```

5. Test the Nginx configuration for syntax errors:

```
1  sudo nginx -t
```

If the test is successful, reload Nginx to apply the changes:

```
1  sudo systemctl reload nginx
```

Advanced Configuration

Beyond basic domain setup, Nginx allows for advanced domain name configurations that can greatly enhance the functionality and security of your web server. These include:

- **HTTPS Configuration:** Setting up SSL/TLS for secure HTTPS connections.

- **WWW Redirection:** Redirecting traffic from the www subdomain to the base domain or vice versa.

- **Custom Error Pages:** Defining custom error pages for different HTTP status codes.

- **Access and Error Logging:** Configuring access and error logs for individual domains.

Each of these advanced configurations require specific directives to be added to your domain's Nginx configuration file. For example, to redirect www requests to the non-www version of your domain, you could add the following server block:

```
1  server {
2      listen 80;
3      server_name www.example.com;
4      return 301 $scheme://example.com$request_uri;
5  }
```

This setup instructs Nginx to listen for requests to `www.example.com` and permanently redirect them to `example.com` using a 301 redirect.

Each of the advanced configurations mentioned serves a particular purpose and can be critical in certain scenarios. It is advisable to explore each configuration in detail to fully understand its implications and best practices for implementation.

Configuring domain names in Nginx is a foundational aspect of web server setup that facilitates the hosting of multiple websites on a single instance. Starting with a basic configuration and gradually implementing more advanced settings as needed can greatly enhance the functionality, performance, and security of your web applications. With careful setup and management, Nginx can serve as a powerful engine behind your web presence.

4.2   SSL/TLS Basics for Web Security

SSL (Secure Sockets Layer) and TLS (Transport Layer Security) are cryptographic protocols designed to provide communication security over a computer network. Their fundamental purpose is to ensure the integrity, confidentiality, and authentication of the data transmitted between a web server and a client. While SSL is the predecessor of TLS, the term SSL continues to be widely used in practice, even when referring to TLS protocols. For the sake of clarity and current relevance, our discussion will focus primarily on TLS while acknowledging its historical roots in SSL.

The mechanism of TLS involves a series of steps that establish a secure session between the server and the client. Initially, the process begins with a "handshake" phase, where the server and client agree on the version of the protocol to use, select cryptographic algorithms, and authenticate the server to the client. Optionally, the client can also be authenticated to the server.

- The first step of the handshake is when the client sends a "ClientHello" message specifying its TLS version, supported cipher suites, and a random byte string for session security.

86

- The server responds with a "ServerHello" message, selecting the protocol version and a cipher suite from the options provided by the client, and sends its own random byte string.

- Next, the server sends its digital certificate to the client for authentication. The certificate contains the server's public key and is issued by a Certificate Authority (CA) that the client trusts.

- The server may request a certificate from the client, if client authentication is required.

- Following the certificate exchange, the server sends a "Server-HelloDone" message, signaling the end of its part of the negotiation.

- The client may respond with a digital certificate if requested. Then, it generates a pre-master secret, encrypts it with the server's public key, and sends it to the server.

- Both the client and the server generate the session keys from the pre-master secret and the random bytes exchanged at the start of the handshake.

- Finally, both sides signal to each other that subsequent records will be protected with the newly negotiated keys, algorithms, and secrets.

Once the handshake is complete, all transmitted data between the server and client is encrypted with the agreed-upon encryption algorithms and keys. This ensures that even if the transmission is intercepted, the data cannot be read or tampered with by the interceptor.

It's worth mentioning the concept of "cipher suites" in the context of TLS. A cipher suite is a combination of cryptographic algorithms used during the TLS/SSL handshake. These algorithms are used for key exchange, digital signatures, and data encryption. The choice of cipher suite can affect the security and performance of the TLS secured communications. Modern versions of TLS, including 1.2 and

1.3, support more secure and efficient cipher suites that are robust against known cryptographic attacks.

Embedding TLS in web server configuration is essential for securing web communications. This involves obtaining a digital certificate from a trusted CA, configuring the web server software (such as Nginx) to use TLS, and enforcing secure connections through redirects and security headers. The next sections will delve into generating SSL certificates, configuring Nginx to use SSL/TLS, and other related configuration tasks.

Ensuring the use of strong cryptography via TLS is a cornerstone of web security. It not only protects data but also builds trust with users by verifying the identity of websites and ensuring the confidentiality and integrity of information exchanged.

4.3   Generating SSL Certificates

Generating SSL certificates is a crucial step in securing web communications between the server and clients. SSL certificates provide a means to encrypt and protect data in transit, thereby enhancing the security posture of web services. This section will guide you through the process of generating a self-signed SSL certificate and obtaining a certificate from a Certificate Authority (CA).

Generating a Self-Signed SSL Certificate

Self-signed certificates are useful for development environments or internal applications where the trustworthiness of the certificate, as verified by a third-party CA, is not required. However, it is important to note that browsers and users might receive warnings when accessing sites with self-signed certificates.

To generate a self-signed SSL certificate, the OpenSSL toolkit can be used. OpenSSL is a robust, full-featured toolkit for the Transport Layer Security (TLS) and Secure Sockets Layer (SSL) protocols. Follow the steps below to create a self-signed certificate:

```
1   # Generate a private key
2   openssl genrsa -out server.key 2048
3
4   # Generate a CSR (Certificate Signing Request)
5   openssl req -new -key server.key -out server.csr
6
7   # Generate the SSL certificate
8   openssl x509 -req -days 365 -in server.csr -signkey server.key -out server.crt
```

server.key is your private key, and server.crt is your newly generated self-signed certificate. The CSR (server.csr) is an intermediate file used in the certificate generation process.

Obtaining a Certificate from a Certificate Authority

For a production environment, it is recommended to use an SSL certificate issued by a recognized CA. This section describes the procedure to obtain a certificate from Let's Encrypt, a popular free Certificate Authority.

Let's Encrypt provides a client called Certbot that automates the process of obtaining and renewing certificates.

```
1   # Install Certbot
2   sudo apt-get update
3   sudo apt-get install certbot
4
5   # Generate the certificate for your domain
6   sudo certbot certonly --standalone -d example.com -d www.example.com
```

Replace example.com with your actual domain name. The certonly option indicates that the certificate will be generated without making any changes to your web server configuration. The --standalone option is used to run a temporary web server on port 80 to complete the domain validation process.

Certbot will generate the following files:

- fullchain.pem: the certificate file

- privkey.pem: the private key

These   files   are   typically   stored   in

/etc/letsencrypt/live/example.com/. You will reference these files in your Nginx configuration to secure your web server, as described in subsequent sections.

Note: It's important to keep in mind that Let's Encrypt certificates have a 90-day validity period. However, with Certbot, renewing certificates automatically is straightforward and can be set up with cron jobs or systemd timers.

Understanding and executing the process of generating SSL certificates, whether self-signed for testing and development or obtained from a CA for production uses, is pivotal in ensuring the security and integrity of data over the web. The next step after obtaining your certificates is configuring Nginx to use these certificates, which will be covered in the following section.

4.4 Configuring Nginx to Use SSL/TLS

Let's start with discussing how to configure Nginx to use SSL/TLS, ensuring that your web applications are secure and that data exchanged between the server and its clients is encrypted. The process involves modifying Nginx configuration files to specify the location of your SSL certificate and its key file. This section assumes that you have already obtained an SSL certificate, as covered in previous sections.

First, locate your Nginx configuration file, which is typically found at /etc/nginx/nginx.conf or within the /etc/nginx/sites-available/ directory for specific domain configurations. You will need to edit this file (or create a new file for your domain under sites-available) to include SSL configuration directives.

Here is a step-by-step guide to enable SSL/TLS for your Nginx server:

- **Step 1:** Open your domain's Nginx configuration file with a text editor. For example, use sudo nano /etc/nginx/sites-available/yourdomain.com.conf.

- **Step 2:** Inside the server block for your domain, add the lines to define the listening port for SSL (typically 443), and specify the location of your SSL certificate and key. Ensure to replace yourdomain.com with your actual domain name.

```
1   server {
2       listen 443 ssl;
3       server_name yourdomain.com;
4
5       ssl_certificate /etc/ssl/certs/yourdomain.com.crt;
6       ssl_certificate_key /etc/ssl/private/yourdomain.com.key;
7
8       ... # Additional configuration settings
9   }
```

- **Step 3:** Optionally, you may want to add SSL configuration settings to enhance security, such as specifying preferred ciphers, protocols, and session settings. For example:

```
1   ssl_protocols TLSv1.2 TLSv1.3;
2   ssl_ciphers HIGH:!aNULL:!MD5;
3   ssl_prefer_server_ciphers on;
4   ssl_session_cache shared:SSL:10m;
5   ssl_session_timeout 10m;
```

It is crucial to stay updated with the best practices for SSL/TLS settings, as recommendations may change over time to counter new vulnerabilities.

- **Step 4:** If you also want to serve content over HTTP (port 80) and redirect it to HTTPS, add a separate server block before or after the SSL server block to handle the redirection:

```
1   server {
2       listen 80;
3       server_name yourdomain.com;
4       return 301 https://$host$request_uri;
5   }
```

This will ensure that any requests made to your domain using HTTP will be automatically redirected to HTTPS.

- **Step 5:** Save your configuration file and test the Nginx configuration for errors with sudo nginx -t. If the test is successful, you can apply the changes by restarting Nginx with   `sudo systemctl reload nginx`   or   `sudo nginx -s reload`.

By following these steps, you have successfully configured your Nginx server to use SSL/TLS, securing the communication between your server and its clients. Keep in mind that maintaining security is an ongoing process. Regularly update your SSL/TLS settings based on current best practices and renew your SSL certificates before they expire to ensure uninterrupted secure service.

4.5   Redirecting HTTP Traffic to HTTPS

Redirecting HTTP traffic to HTTPS is a critical step in ensuring that all communications between your web server and the clients are encrypted. This process involves configuring Nginx to listen for incoming connections on the standard HTTP port (port 80) and then redirecting those requests to HTTPS, which listens on port 443. This ensures that even if a user attempts to access the website using the insecure HTTP protocol, they are automatically upgraded to the secure HTTPS protocol.

To achieve this redirection in Nginx, the configuration file for the server block handling HTTP requests needs to be modified. This involves using the `server` directive to define the conditions under which the redirection occurs. Below is a step-by-step guide to configuring Nginx to perform this redirection:

1. Open the Nginx configuration file for the site that you want to redirect from HTTP to HTTPS. This file is typically located at `/etc/nginx/sites-available/yourdomain.com`.

2. Inside the `server` block that listens on port 80 for HTTP traffic, add a `return` directive which specifies the return code and the URL to redirect to. A return code of 301 is used for a permanent redirect.

3. The URL in the `return` directive should be the HTTPS version

of your site. Ensure that you include `https://` before your domain name.

Here is an example configuration snippet that illustrates how to redirect HTTP traffic to HTTPS:

```
1  server {
2      listen 80;
3      server_name yourdomain.com www.yourdomain.com;
4
5      return 301 https://$server_name$request_uri;
6  }
```

This configuration listens for HTTP requests on port 80. When a request is received, it permanently redirects the client to the HTTPS version of the site, preserving the original request URI. The `$server_name` variable is used to dynamically insert the server name, and `$request_uri` appends the original requested URI to the redirect URL, ensuring that specific page requests are maintained through the redirect process.

Once this configuration is in place, it is essential to test the configuration and reload Nginx to apply the changes. This can be done with the following commands:

```
sudo nginx -t
sudo systemctl reload nginx
```

After reloading Nginx, all HTTP traffic should be seamlessly redirected to HTTPS, significantly increasing the security of communications between your web server and clients by ensuring they are encrypted. This is not only beneficial for security but also favorably impacts search engine rankings and user trust.

4.6 Working with Let's Encrypt for Free SSL/TLS Certificates

Let's Encrypt represents a paradigm shift in web security, offering cost-free, automated, and open Certificate Authority (CA) services.

This initiative simplifies the process of securing web traffic by enabling website owners to obtain SSL/TLS certificates without facing complex procedures or prohibitive costs.

Obtaining a certificate from Let's Encrypt can be streamlined into a few straightforward steps when using Nginx as the web server. These steps involve the use of Certbot, an open-source software tool that automates the process of obtaining and renewing Let's Encrypt SSL certificates.

- First, ensure that your server environment meets the prerequisites for installing Certbot. This includes having root access to your server and ensuring that your version of Nginx is up-to-date.

- Next, install Certbot and its Nginx plugin. Depending on your operating system, the installation commands will vary. For most Linux distributions, the following commands are applicable:

```
1    sudo apt update
2    sudo apt install certbot python3-certbot-nginx
```

- Once Certbot is installed, you can proceed to obtain an SSL/TLS certificate by running:

```
1    sudo certbot --nginx
```

  During this step, Certbot will prompt you to provide an email address for important account notifications, agree to the terms of service, and select which domains to activate HTTPS for.

- Certbot will then automatically update your Nginx configuration to use the newly obtained SSL/TLS certificate and set up a renewal process that renews the certificate before it expires.

After successfully obtaining and configuring SSL/TLS certificates with Certbot, it's essential to verify that HTTPS is properly enabled and configured on your website. You can do this by accessing your site via a web browser using "https://" before your domain name.

Let's Encrypt certificates have a 90-day expiration period. Fortunately, Certbot handles the renewal process automatically. To test the automated renewal process, you can simulate a renewal attempt with the following command:

```
1   sudo certbot renew --dry-run
```

In addition to automating the process of obtaining and renewing certificates, Certbot can also help configure more advanced SSL/TLS settings to enhance the security of your web server. For example, you can improve the security of your server by setting up stricter SSL protocols and ciphers. This involves manually editing the Nginx configuration file for your domain, a process that requires a comprehensive understanding of SSL/TLS best practices.

Working with Let's Encrypt and Certbot markedly enhances the security of web servers running Nginx by streamlining the process of securing web communications. By leveraging these tools, developers and website administrators can ensure their web applications operate securely, without the burden of complicated certificate management processes or the high costs typically associated with SSL/TLS certificates.

4.7 Fine-Tuning SSL/TLS Settings for Enhanced Security

Fine-tuning SSL/TLS settings in Nginx enhances web server security tremendously. SSL/TLS configuration goes beyond basic setup; it involves optimizing security protocols, cipher suites, and various other settings. This section discusses the detailed steps to achieve a more secure SSL/TLS setup.

Firstly, it's imperative to restrict the use of outdated and less secure SSL/TLS protocols. Only TLS versions 1.2 and 1.3 should be enabled, as they provide stronger security measures. To achieve this, add the following directive to your Nginx configuration file:

```
1   ssl_protocols TLSv1.2 TLSv1.3;
```

Next, we need to consider the cipher suites. Cipher suites are sets of algorithms that define how data is encrypted. Nginx allows you to specify which cipher suites to use, prioritizing more secure ones. Here's an example of how to specify secure cipher suites in your Nginx configuration:

```
ssl_ciphers 'ECDHE-ECDSA-AES256-GCM-SHA384:ECDHE-RSA-AES256-GCM-SHA384:
            ECDHE-ECDSA-CHACHA20-POLY1305:ECDHE-RSA-CHACHA20-POLY1305:
            ECDHE-ECDSA-AES128-GCM-SHA256:ECDHE-RSA-AES128-GCM-SHA256:
            HIGH:!aNULL:!eNULL:!EXPORT:!DES:!MD5:!PSK:!RC4';
```

Such configuration ensures the use of strong and secure cipher suites, thus enhancing the security of the SSL/TLS connections.

To further secure the SSL/TLS setup, enabling Strict Transport Security (HSTS) is crucial. HSTS informs browsers that your site must be accessed using HTTPS only. This can be achieved by adding the following to your server block:

```
add_header Strict-Transport-Security "max-age=31536000; includeSubDomains"
          always;
```

This setting tells browsers that for the next year (31536000 seconds), they should automatically convert all links to HTTPS.

Another significant step is to enhance the Diffie-Hellman key exchange process's security. It's recommended to use a strong, unique Diffie-Hellman group, which can be generated as follows:

```
openssl dhparam -out /etc/ssl/certs/dhparam.pem 2048
```

After generating the file, you need to add the following directive to your Nginx configuration to use the newly generated Diffie-Hellman parameter:

```
ssl_dhparam /etc/ssl/certs/dhparam.pem;
```

Following these steps, your SSL/TLS configuration will be significantly more secure. However, it is essential to test your configuration to ensure no vulnerabilities are present. Tools like SSL Labs' SSL Test can analyze your web server's SSL/TLS configuration and highlight any potential security issues.

Fine-tuning SSL/TLS settings in Nginx is not merely about enabling

SSL/TLS but about configuring it in a way that maximizes security. By setting appropriate protocols, cipher suites, implementing HSTS, and using strong Diffie-Hellman parameters, the security of communication between clients and the server is significantly enhanced. Regular testing and updating of these configurations are equally important to adapt to emerging security threats and vulnerabilities.

4.8 HTTP/2 Support and Configuration

HTTP/2 is a major revision of the HTTP network protocol used by the World Wide Web. It focuses on performance; specifically, end-user perceived latency, network and server resource usage. One major goal is to allow the use of a single connection from browsers to a website, a contrast to HTTP/1.x, which opens a new connection for each resource. Nginx, being a high-performance web server, offers support for HTTP/2, bringing improvements in the efficiency, speed, and security of web applications.

Enabling HTTP/2 in Nginx requires minimal configuration, but it requires that connections be secured with SSL/TLS, as most modern browsers support HTTP/2 only over HTTPS. This section explores the steps involved in configuring Nginx to support HTTP/2, enhancing the performance and security of web applications.

Prerequisites for HTTP/2 in Nginx

Before enabling HTTP/2, ensure that:

- Nginx is compiled with the `--with-http_v2_module` directive. This is typically enabled by default in most pre-compiled packages available today.

- SSL/TLS is configured for your domain, as HTTP/2 requires an encrypted connection.

Configuring Nginx for HTTP/2

The configuration of HTTP/2 in Nginx is straightforward. The following steps outline the process:

- Open the Nginx configuration file for your site, usually located at /etc/nginx/sites-available/your_domain.

- Find the server block for your SSL-enabled site. It typically listens on port 443.

- Add the http2 parameter to the listen directive within this server block. It should look something like this:

```
server {
    listen 443 ssl http2;
    server_name your_domain.com;

    # SSL configuration
    ssl_certificate /path/to/your/certificate.pem;
    ssl_certificate_key /path/to/your/private.key;

    # Other configurations
}
```

This directive informs Nginx to enable HTTP/2 for this server block. Note that only adding the http2 parameter to the listen directive is necessary, as the existing SSL configurations remain applicable.

Verifying HTTP/2 Configuration

After applying the changes in your Nginx configuration, it's crucial to verify the successful activation of HTTP/2 on your web server. Use the following command to reload Nginx and apply the new configuration:

```
sudo systemctl reload nginx
```

To confirm that HTTP/2 is working, you can use browser developer tools or command-line tools like curl. The following curl command can be used to check the response headers:

```
1   curl -I --http2 https://your_domain.com
```

If HTTP/2 is enabled correctly, you will see a response similar to the following:

```
HTTP/2 200
...
```

The presence of HTTP/2 at the beginning of the response indicates that HTTP/2 is successfully enabled for your site.

Performance Considerations

While HTTP/2 significantly enhances performance by reducing latency and allowing multiplexing, enabling it alongside SSL/TLS introduces computational overhead due to encryption. However, the performance benefits of HTTP/2 usually outweigh the slight overhead introduced by SSL/TLS, especially for websites serving numerous resources (CSS, JavaScript, images) over a single connection.

Integrating HTTP/2 into Nginx setups not only provides performance benefits but also encourages the use of HTTPS, contributing to a more secure web. By following the steps outlined above, administrators can enable HTTP/2 on their Nginx servers, leveraging faster load times and improved user experience.

4.9 Managing Multiple Domains and Subdomains

Nginx, a powerful and efficient web server, emerges as a superior choice for managing multiple domains and subdomains. It enables administrators to host several websites on a single server instance, thus optimizing resource utilization and simplifying server management. This efficiency is paramount in today's diversified and domain-intensive web environments.

To start, domain and subdomain management in Nginx is primarily configured through server blocks (often referred to as virtual hosts in Apache). These server blocks allow Nginx to distinguish between incoming requests for different domains and serve the appropriate content. Essential directives and their configurations are outlined below, emphasizing their role in multi-domain and subdomain management.

- `listen` - Specifies the port number and IP address on which the server block will accept incoming requests. For standard web traffic, port 80 is used, and for encrypted traffic (SSL/TLS), port 443 is specified.

- `server_name` - Defines the domain or subdomain names that the server block is responsible for. Wildcards can be used for subdomain management, for instance, `*.example.com` will match any subdomain of `example.com`.

- `root` - Determines the directory from which Nginx serves files for the server block. This directive is crucial for directing to the correct website data for each domain or subdomain.

- `index` - Specifies the files that Nginx should use as the index page for a directory. Common configurations include `index.html`, `index.php`, etc.

To illustrate, consider the following example where two domains, `example.com` and `anotherexample.com`, are configured on the same Nginx server:

```
1   server {
2       listen 80;
3       server_name example.com www.example.com;
4
5       root /var/www/example;
6       index index.html index.htm;
7   }
8
9   server {
10      listen 80;
11      server_name anotherexample.com www.anotherexample.com;
12
13      root /var/www/anotherexample;
14      index index.html index.htm;
```

```
15  }
```

In this configuration, requests to either example.com or www.example.com will be directed to the content stored in /var/www/example, and similarly for anotherexample.com. This delineation allows for effective management of multiple domains.

Subdomains follow a similar configuration pattern, with an emphasis on the server_name directive to specify each subdomain. Wildcard certificates and server names are often utilized for scalability and simplification of SSL certificate management across subdomains.

For enhanced performance and security, each server block can and should be further customized with SSL/TLS configurations, location blocks for handling specific request URLs, and other directives catering to caching, redirections, and compression. It is also recommended to leverage the include directive to modularize configuration for maintainability and clarity.

Managing multiple domains and subdomains in Nginx involves a concise understanding and application of server blocks, alongside the pertinent directives such as listen, server_name, root, and index. With Nginx's efficient architecture, administrators can ensure optimal performance, security, and resource utilization across a diverse web ecosystem.

4.10 Securing Web Applications with Content Security Policies

Content Security Policy (CSP) is a security standard introduced to prevent Cross-Site Scripting (XSS), clickjacking, and other code injection attacks resulting from the execution of malicious content in the trusted web page context. With Nginx, implementing CSP headers can significantly enhance the security of web applications. This section will discuss the methodology to configure CSP in Nginx and its implications for web application security.

To begin, the CSP header is declared in the HTTP response sent from the server to the client. It specifies which dynamic resources are allowed to load and execute in the browser, thereby mitigating the risk of executing malicious scripts. The foundation of configuring CSP in Nginx involves the add_header directive. This directive allows the addition of arbitrary header fields to an HTTP response header, making it suitable for specifying a CSP policy.

The following snippet illustrates the basic syntax for including a CSP header in an Nginx configuration file:

```
1  server {
2    listen 80;
3    server_name example.com;
4
5    add_header Content-Security-Policy "default-src 'self'; script-src 'self'
        https://trustedscripts.example.com";
6  }
```

In this example, the CSP policy restricts the sources for various content types. The 'default-src 'self'' directive restricts all content sources to the same origin as the document. This implies that any attempts to load resources from domains other than example.com will be blocked, unless explicitly allowed. The 'script-src' directive further refines these restrictions for scripts, allowing scripts to be loaded from the site's own domain and the specified trusted domain.

Implementing CSP in Nginx requires careful crafting of the policy to balance security and functionality. A restrictive CSP can enhance security, but may inadvertently block legitimate content, breaking site functionality. Conversely, a too-permissive policy might not offer sufficient protection against attacks. Testing the CSP thoroughly in a development environment before deploying to production is crucial to identify and resolve such conflicts.

Management and maintenance of CSPs involve constant monitoring and updating as the web application evolves. The reporting features of CSP are instrumental for this purpose. By specifying a report URI in the CSP header, like so:

```
1  add_header Content-Security-Policy "default-src 'self'; script-src 'self' https
        ://trustedscripts.example.com; report-uri /csp-report-endpoint/";
```

the browser will send reports in JSON format to the specified URI whenever a violation of the CSP occurs. This reporting mechanism is invaluable for detecting and responding to attempted attacks, as well as for identifying legitimate content that may have been inadvertently blocked by the CSP.

Integrating CSP with Nginx enhances the security posture of web applications by offering a robust mechanism against common web vulnerabilities. However, it is not a silver bullet. CSP should be part of a comprehensive security strategy, complemented by other security practices and mechanisms such as secure coding, regular security audits, and the use of HTTPS.

4.11 Performance   Considerations   for SSL/TLS

Implementing SSL/TLS encryption in Nginx is pivotal for enhancing the security of web communications. However, administrators must be aware of the performance implications that come with secure connections. SSL/TLS operations involve computationally intensive processes, such as the exchange of cryptographic keys and the encryption and decryption of transferred data. These processes can introduce latency and increase server load, affecting the overall response time perceived by end-users.

To manage these performance considerations effectively, several strategies can be employed. These include optimizing SSL/TLS configuration, leveraging session reuse, selecting efficient cryptographic algorithms, and employing hardware acceleration where possible.

- **Optimizing SSL/TLS Configuration**: Minimizing the SSL/TLS handshake overhead can significantly improve performance. This can be achieved by enabling session resumption features like session IDs and TLS tickets in the Nginx configuration. Session resumption allows clients to reuse previously negotiated security parameters without going through the full handshake process again, reducing latency and server load.

- **Leveraging Session Reuse**:   Implementing session reuse mechanisms is crucial for reducing the number of handshakes performed by the server.   Nginx supports both Session IDs and Session Tickets for this purpose. Enabling these features can be done by including the appropriate directives in the SSL module configuration block.

```
1  ssl_session_cache shared:SSL:10m;
2  ssl_session_timeout 10m;
3  ssl_session_tickets on;
```

- **Selecting Efficient Cryptographic Algorithms**: The choice of cryptographic algorithms can impact the performance of SSL/TLS.   Algorithms   with   higher   computational requirements can introduce more latency compared to those that are more efficient.   For instance, Elliptic Curve Cryptography (ECC) can provide the same level of security as RSA with much shorter key lengths, resulting in faster operations. Therefore, configuring Nginx to prefer ECC over RSA where possible can enhance performance.

```
1  ssl_prefer_server_ciphers on;
2  ssl_ciphers 'ECDHE-ECDSA-AES128-GCM-SHA256:ECDHE-RSA-AES128-GCM-SHA256';
```

- **Employing Hardware Acceleration**:   Some servers are equipped with hardware specifically designed to accelerate cryptographic operations.   Utilizing such hardware can offload the computational burden from the CPU, enhancing the capacity to handle SSL/TLS connections.   Configuring Nginx to take advantage of hardware acceleration involves specifying the appropriate engine in the SSL configuration.

These strategies highlight the balance that must be struck between securing web communications through SSL/TLS and maintaining optimal server performance. By carefully configuring SSL/TLS settings in Nginx and leveraging available optimization techniques, administrators can secure their web applications without significantly detracting from the user experience.

104

In addition to these server-side optimizations, administrators should also consider client-side performance. Modern browsers have optimizations for handling SSL/TLS connections, but excessive SSL/TLS handshakes can still lead to noticeable latency. Thus, ensuring that web applications make efficient use of persistent connections and proper caching strategies can further improve performance from the end-user's perspective.

To assess the impact of SSL/TLS on performance, administrators can utilize tools such as SSL Labs' SSL Test to evaluate the efficiency of their SSL/TLS configurations. Furthermore, monitoring server metrics under load can offer insights into the real-world performance implications of SSL/TLS, enabling ongoing optimization efforts.

While implementing SSL/TLS is essential for securing Nginx web servers, it is equally important to consider the performance implications. Through careful configuration and optimization of SSL/TLS settings, administrators can ensure that the security enhancements do not compromise the responsiveness and scalability of their web services.

4.12 Troubleshooting Common SSL/TLS Issues

In this section, we will discuss traditional hurdles encountered while implementing Secure Sockets Layer (SSL) and Transport Layer Security (TLS) protocols with Nginx. Although the intention behind SSL/TLS is to secure data transmission, misconfigurations can result in errors that might confuse or intimidate. The following are common SSL/TLS issues, with explanations and solutions to adequately address them.

- **Expired Certificates**: A prevalent issue is the expiration of SSL/TLS certificates. When a certificate expires, browsers will warn users away from the site, significantly impacting its accessibility and trustworthiness.

  Solution: Regularly check the expiration dates of your

105

certificates. A viable method to automate renewals and avoid downtime due to expired certificates is to employ tools like `certbot` from Let's Encrypt, which can automatically renew certificates before they expire.

- **Insecure Cipher Suites**: Utilization of outdated or insecure cipher suites can undermine the security of SSL/TLS connections. Modern browsers will display a warning or prevent access to sites using such suites, as they are susceptible to attacks.

  Solution: Update your Nginx configuration to include only strong cipher suites. Use the `ssl_cipher` directive within your server block to specify a list of desired ciphers. Online resources such as Mozilla's SSL Configuration Generator can help select up-to-date and secure options.

- **SSL Handshake Failures**: These failures occur when the server and client cannot establish a secure connection. Causes might range from server misconfigurations to client-side issues.

  Solution: Ensure that your `ssl_certificate` and `ssl_certificate_key` directives are correctly specified with valid paths to your certificate and private key files, respectively. Additionally, verify that the client supports the cipher suites and SSL/TLS protocol versions offered by the server.

- **Missing Intermediate Certificates**: Occasionally, systems will report errors about a missing or incomplete certificate chain. This usually happens when intermediate certificates are not properly configured.

  Solution: Concatenate your server's certificate file with the intermediate certificates from your CA (Certificate Authority) into a single file. The correct order places your server's certificate first, followed by the intermediate certificates. Update the `ssl_certificate` directive to point to this concatenated file.

106

- **Performance Issues with SSL/TLS**: Enabling SSL/TLS encryption can introduce computational overhead, potentially affecting server performance and response times.

  Solution: Implement performance-optimization techniques such as session caching and session tickets. The `ssl_session_cache` and `ssl_session_tickets` directives in Nginx allow for these optimizations, reducing the SSL/TLS handshake overhead for subsequent secure connections.

Addressing these common issues can significantly enhance the reliability, security, and performance of SSL/TLS configurations in Nginx. For further troubleshooting, Nginx's error logs (`/var/log/nginx/error.log`) provide valuable insights into issues and their potential resolutions. Remember, maintaining a secure configuration involves regular reviews and updates to adapt to emerging security standards and threat landscapes.

Chapter 5

Reverse Proxy and Load Balancing

Utilizing Nginx for reverse proxying and load balancing enables efficient distribution of incoming network traffic across multiple servers, enhancing the performance, reliability, and scalability of web applications. As a reverse proxy, Nginx acts as an intermediary for requests from clients, forwarding them to backend servers, and then delivering the servers' responses back to the clients. Load balancing, on the other hand, involves the dynamic distribution of client requests or network load across several servers, ensuring no single server becomes overwhelmed. This configuration maximizes uptime, optimizes resource utilization, and improves overall user experience by reducing response times.

5.1 Introduction to Reverse Proxying with Nginx

Reverse proxying with Nginx involves configuring Nginx as an intermediary between client requests and one or more servers.

When a client sends a request to the Nginx server, Nginx forwards the request to a specified backend server. Upon receiving the response from the backend server, Nginx then forwards this response back to the client. This process not only hides the identity of the backend servers but also provides a layer of abstraction and control to enhance security, manage loads, and improve the overall performance of web applications.

Setting up Nginx as a reverse proxy involves several strategic steps, beginning with the installation of Nginx on a server that is accessible by clients. The configuration file for Nginx, typically found at /etc/nginx/nginx.conf, is then edited to define the reverse proxy settings. Within this configuration file, a server block is established to listen on a specific port, and within this server block, a location block is used to specify the proxying behavior.

The primary directive used in the configuration of a reverse proxy setup is proxy_pass. This directive informs Nginx of the backend server's URL to which the request should be forwarded. The syntax for the proxy_pass directive is straightforward:

```
1  location / {
2      proxy_pass http://backend_server_address;
3  }
```

In this example, any request that matches the location block (in this case, any request) will be forwarded to the specified backend server URL. It's crucial to ensure that the backend server address is correctly specified, as any error in the address can lead to failed requests or incorrect routing.

In addition to proxy_pass, there are several other directives that enhance the functionality and control of the reverse proxy setup. These include:

- proxy_set_header - Used to modify or add headers to the request sent to the backend server.

- proxy_redirect - Adjusts the location header fields in responses from the backend server.

- proxy_buffering - Enables or disables buffering of responses

110

from the proxyed server.

- `proxy_cache` - Defines the caching behavior, including specifying which responses should be cached.

Configuring a reverse proxy also involves consideration for the underlying network infrastructure and the specific requirements of the web application. Security settings, including SSL/TLS termination, need to be integrated into the reverse proxy configuration to safeguard data in transit. Additionally, load balancing strategies can be incorporated within the reverse proxy setup to distribute the load among multiple backend servers, enhancing the scalability and reliability of the application.

This section has introduced the concept of reverse proxying with Nginx, highlighted the importance of the `proxy_pass` directive, and outlined additional configuration directives that play a significant role in tailoring the reverse proxy setup to meet specific application needs. The subsequent sections will delve deeper into setting up Nginx as a reverse proxy, examining load balancing techniques, SSL/TLS configurations, and troubleshooting common issues encountered in reverse proxy and load balancing configurations.

5.2 Setting Up Nginx as a Reverse Proxy

Configuring Nginx to serve as a reverse proxy involves a series of steps that are straightforward yet require precision. At its core, setting up Nginx as a reverse proxy allows it to accept client requests, forward them to one or more backend servers, and return the response from the backend server to the client. This mechanism not only improves the speed and efficiency of your web applications but also enhances security and scalability.

To begin, ensure that Nginx is installed on your system. If not, you can usually install it using your operating system's package manager. For instance, on a Ubuntu system, you would use the command `sudo apt-get install nginx`.

Once Nginx is installed, the main configuration file, typically found at /etc/nginx/nginx.conf, needs to be edited to define how requests to your server should be handled. However, for simplicity and maintainability, it is recommended to place reverse proxy configurations in separate files inside the /etc/nginx/sites-available/ directory, and then create symbolic links to those files in the /etc/nginx/sites-enabled/ directory.

A basic reverse proxy setup can be defined as follows:

```
server {
    listen 80;

    server_name example.com;

    location / {
        proxy_pass http://your_backend_server_ip_or_domain;
        proxy_set_header Host $host;
        proxy_set_header X-Real-IP $remote_addr;
        proxy_set_header X-Forwarded-For $proxy_add_x_forwarded_for;
        proxy_set_header X-Forwarded-Proto $scheme;
    }
}
```

In this configuration:

- listen 80; tells Nginx to listen on port 80, which is the default port for HTTP traffic.

- server_name example.com; specifies the domain name of the site being served by this server block.

- The location / {...} block defines how to respond to requests for the root URL. Inside this block:

  - proxy_pass http://your_backend_server_ip_or_domain; directs Nginx to forward the request to the specified backend server.

  - proxy_set_header directives are used to modify or add headers to the request forwarded to the backend server. This is crucial for the backend server to understand the original context of the request.

After updating the configuration, test to ensure there are no syntax errors using `sudo nginx -t`. If the test is successful, reload Nginx to apply the changes:

```
1  sudo systemctl reload nginx
```

This basic setup demonstrates how to configure Nginx as a reverse proxy. However, numerous additional parameters and directives can be used to tailor the behavior to your specific needs, such as load balancing, caching, and handling WebSocket connections. Monitoring and logging settings should also be considered to maintain insight into the performance and health of your Nginx server in its role as a reverse proxy.

5.3 Load Balancing Techniques in Nginx

Load balancing in Nginx is an essential technique for distributing incoming network traffic across multiple backend servers, known as an upstream server pool. This mechanism ensures that no single server bears too much load, thereby increasing the reliability, efficiency, and scalability of web services. Nginx supports several load balancing methods, each with unique characteristics and use cases. This section will discuss the primary techniques, including round-robin, least connections, and IP hash.

Round-Robin Load Balancing

The round-robin method is the default load balancing algorithm utilized by Nginx. It distributes incoming client requests sequentially across the server pool. When the end of the list is reached, the process repeats from the first server. This method does not account for the current load or the number of active connections to the backend servers. To enable round-robin load balancing, the server configuration within an upstream block should resemble the following:

```
1  upstream backend {
2      server backend1.example.com;
3      server backend2.example.com;
```

113

```
4       server backend3.example.com;
5   }
```

This configuration implies an equal distribution of traffic across the three backend servers listed. However, it is possible to assign a weight to each server to distribute the load unevenly based on the server's capacity.

```
1   upstream backend {
2       server backend1.example.com weight=3;
3       server backend2.example.com weight=2;
4       server backend3.example.com weight=1;
5   }
```

In this adjusted configuration, the backend1.example.com server will receive a larger share of the incoming requests compared to backend3.example.com.

Least Connections Load Balancing

The least connections method dynamically distributes incoming requests to the server with the fewest active connections. This approach is particularly effective in environments where session persistence is essential, or the request load is unevenly distributed. Configuration for least connections load balancing modifies the upstream block as follows:

```
1   upstream backend {
2       least_conn;
3       server backend1.example.com;
4       server backend2.example.com;
5       server backend3.example.com;
6   }
```

IP Hash Load Balancing

The IP hash method of load balancing ensures that requests from the same client IP address are consistently routed to the same backend server. This is crucial for session persistence, guaranteeing that a user's session is maintained with the same server for subsequent requests. The configuration for IP hash load balancing is achieved by altering the upstream block in the following manner:

```
1  upstream backend {
2      ip_hash;
3      server backend1.example.com;
4      server backend2.example.com;
5      server backend3.example.com;
6  }
```

This configuration ensures that the IP address of the client is hashed and transformed into a unique identifier to select the backend server. This process retains client-to-server mapping persistently, allowing for a consistent experience.

Each of these load balancing techniques offers unique benefits tailored to specific application requirements. The choice of technique depends on the nature of the web application, the expected traffic patterns, and the necessity for session persistence. Adjusting the configuration of Nginx to employ these techniques can significantly enhance the performance, reliability, and scalability of web services.

5.4 Configuring Upstream Servers for Load Balancing

Configuring upstream servers in Nginx for load balancing involves defining a group of servers amongst which traffic will be distributed. This configuration is pivotal for ensuring high availability and scalability of web applications by dispersing the load effectively.

To begin with, the upstream module in Nginx needs to be utilized. The upstream module allows for the declaration of a server group under a custom name, and subsequent proxy_pass directives can refer to this group. A basic configuration example is as follows:

```
1  upstream myapp {
2      server backend1.example.com;
3      server backend2.example.com;
4  }
```

In the example above, 'myapp' represents the name of the upstream group, which consists of two servers: 'backend1.example.com' and 'backend2.example.com'.   When Nginx processes a request that matches a location configured to proxy to 'myapp', it will forward the request to one of the servers listed under the 'myapp' upstream directive.

Load balancing methods play a crucial role in how requests are distributed among the servers in an upstream group. By default, Nginx uses a round-robin approach, where each server is selected in turn based on their defined order.   However, Nginx supports several other methods that can be specified using the 'least_conn' and 'ip_hash' directives to handle different load distribution requirements:

```
1  upstream myapp {
2      least_conn;
3      server backend1.example.com;
4      server backend2.example.com;
5  }
```

In the configuration above, the 'least_conn' directive instructs Nginx to forward requests to the server with the least number of active connections, which is a more adaptive load balancing method compared to round-robin.

Moreover, it's essential to account for the possibility of server failures. The 'max_fails' and 'fail_timeout' parameters allow for the configuration of how Nginx should respond to unresponsive servers:

```
1  upstream myapp {
2      server backend1.example.com max_fails=2 fail_timeout=30s;
3      server backend2.example.com;
4  }
```

In this setup, if 'backend1.example.com' fails to respond after two attempts within a 30-second window ('fail_timeout'), Nginx will temporarily stop sending requests to that server.

To optimize the usage of upstream servers, several other directives can be employed, such as 'weight', for distributing requests unevenly across servers, and 'hash', for sticky sessions when the 'ip_hash' method does not suffice.

Furthermore, implementing SSL/TLS between Nginx and the upstream servers is critical for secure data transmission. This requires additional directives within the upstream block to specify the use of SSL and the necessary certificate files:

```
upstream myapp {
    server backend1.example.com:443;
    server backend2.example.com:443;

    ssl on;
    ssl_certificate /path/to/certificate.pem;
    ssl_certificate_key /path/to/key.pem;
}
```

By properly configuring upstream servers, Nginx can efficiently manage load balancing to ensure that web applications remain scalable, reliable, and available. This configuration, alongside the utilization of various load balancing techniques and parameters, enables Nginx to serve as a robust, dynamic load balancer.

5.5 Load Balancing Algorithms and Their Configurations

Load balancing is a critical component in optimizing the performance and reliability of web applications by distributing incoming traffic across multiple backend servers. Nginx supports several load balancing algorithms, each suitable for different scenarios and purposes. This section will focus on describing these algorithms and how to configure them in Nginx.

Round-Robin Load Balancing

The Round-Robin algorithm is the simplest form of load balancing and is used by Nginx by default. It distributes incoming requests sequentially among the servers in the upstream group. The main advantage of this algorithm is its simplicity, as it does not require any additional configuration.

```
1   http {
2       upstream backend {
3           server backend1.example.com;
4           server backend2.example.com;
5       }
6
7       server {
8           location / {
9               proxy_pass http://backend;
10          }
11      }
12  }
```

Least Connections

The Least Connections algorithm directs new requests to the server with the fewest active connections. This algorithm is beneficial in scenarios where the request load varies significantly between the servers, or when the servers have differing capacities.

```
1   http {
2       upstream backend {
3           least_conn;
4           server backend1.example.com;
5           server backend2.example.com;
6       }
7
8       server {
9           location / {
10              proxy_pass http://backend;
11          }
12      }
13  }
```

IP Hash

The IP Hash algorithm ensures that requests from the same client IP address are always forwarded to the same server as long as it is available. This can be crucial for maintaining session persistence in applications where it is essential for the client to connect to the same server for each request.

```
1   http {
2       upstream backend {
```

```
3        ip_hash;
4        server backend1.example.com;
5        server backend2.example.com;
6    }
7
8    server {
9        location / {
10            proxy_pass http://backend;
11        }
12    }
13 }
```

Weighted Load Balancing

In situations where the servers in the upstream group have varying capacities, it may be desirable to distribute the load unevenly. This can be achieved using weighted load balancing, where each server is assigned a weight representing its capacity.

```
1  http {
2      upstream backend {
3          server backend1.example.com weight=3;
4          server backend2.example.com weight=1;
5      }
6
7      server {
8          location / {
9              proxy_pass http://backend;
10          }
11      }
12 }
```

The weight parameter denotes the server's capacity relative to the others in the group. Requests will be distributed based on these weights.

Health Checks and Failover Strategies

In addition to the load balancing algorithms, Nginx allows for the configuration of health checks and failover strategies. These mechanisms ensure that traffic is only routed to healthy servers, thereby improving the reliability of the service.

```
1  http {
```

```
2   upstream backend {
3       server backend1.example.com;
4       server backend2.example.com;
5       check interval=3000 rise=2 fall=5 timeout=1000;
6   }
7
8   server {
9       location / {
10          proxy_pass http://backend;
11      }
12  }
13 }
```

Here, check defines the parameters for health checks, with interval specifying the time between checks, rise and fall determining when a server is considered healthy or unhealthy, and timeout setting the maximum duration for a health check.

By understanding and utilizing these load balancing algorithms, you can significantly enhance the performance, reliability, and scalability of your web applications. Proper configuration and tuning according to your specific requirements and traffic patterns are crucial for optimizing the benefits of load balancing with Nginx.

5.6   Health Checks and Failover Strategies

Implementing health checks and failover strategies in Nginx enhances the reliability and availability of web services, ensuring that client requests are served without interruptions even when some backend servers become unavailable. In this context, health checks allow Nginx to continuously monitor the status of the backend servers, while failover strategies dictate how Nginx responds to a server failure, either by rerouting the traffic to healthy servers or by attempting reconnection based on predefined rules.

Configuring Health Checks in Nginx

Health checks in Nginx are performed through the ngx_http_upstream_module, which periodically sends requests to each server in the upstream group to assess its status. To configure health checks, you must define a location that points to a health check file or script on the backend server, which returns an HTTP status code to indicate the server's health.

```
1  upstream backend {
2      server backend1.example.com;
3      server backend2.example.com;
4
5      check interval=3000 rise=2 fall=5 timeout=1000 type=http;
6      check_http_send "GET /health HTTP/1.0\r\n\r\n";
7      check_http_expect_alive http_2xx http_3xx;
8  }
```

In the above configuration, Nginx is instructed to perform a health check every 3000 milliseconds (3 seconds) on each server. A server is considered healthy if it responds with a 2xx or 3xx HTTP status code to the health check request twice (rise=2) consecutively. Conversely, it is marked as failed after five (fall=5) consecutive health check failures. The timeout=1000 specifies that the health check request will timeout after 1000 milliseconds (1 second) if no response is received.

Failover Strategies

Failover strategies in Nginx ensure that traffic is rerouted to healthy servers when one or more backend servers fail. This is inherently supported by Nginx's load balancing mechanism, which only forwards requests to servers marked as healthy. For more nuanced failover handling, you can configure Nginx with backup servers or use the max_fails and fail_timeout parameters.

```
1  upstream backend {
2      server backend1.example.com;
3      server backend2.example.com max_fails=3 fail_timeout=30s;
4      server backend3.example.com backup;
5  }
```

In this configuration, backend2.example.com is removed from the pool of servers if it fails three times (max_fails=3) within a 30-second window (fail_timeout=30s). Additionally, backend3.example.com is designated as a backup server, which means it will only receive traffic if all other non-backup servers are considered unhealthy or

121

unavailable.

Best Practices for Health Checks and Failover Strategies

When implementing health checks and failover strategies in Nginx, consider the following best practices:

- Use lightweight and fast-responding health checks to minimize the impact on server performance.

- Adjust the health check frequency and failover thresholds according to the specific application's tolerance for downtime and performance.

- Regularly review and update the health check endpoint to ensure it accurately reflects the health of the application.

- Consider the use of passive health checks, which rely on monitoring the responses to actual client requests, as a complementary strategy to active health checks.

- In a highly dynamic environment, consider integrating Nginx with a service discovery mechanism to automate the addition and removal of servers in the pool.

Properly configuring health checks and failover strategies is essential for maintaining high availability and reliability of services behind an Nginx reverse proxy or load balancer. By continuously monitoring the health of backend servers and intelligently routing traffic in response to failures, Nginx can significantly reduce service disruptions and enhance the overall user experience.

5.7   SSL/TLS Termination and Pass-Through

SSL/TLS termination and pass-through are critical components of secure web communication in Nginx configurations. These processes significantly influence how encrypted traffic is handled, thereby affecting security and performance. This section will elucidate the implementation and configuration of both SSL/TLS termination and pass-through in Nginx, providing practical insights for optimal setup.

SSL/TLS termination refers to the process where the SSL/TLS session is decrypted at the Nginx reverse proxy. The decrypted traffic is then forwarded to the backend servers as plain HTTP. This approach reduces the encryption overhead on the backend servers, allowing them to focus on delivering content. On the other hand, SSL/TLS pass-through entails forwarding encrypted requests directly to the backend servers, leaving the decryption task to them. This method maintains end-to-end encryption but requires backend servers to handle decryption, impacting their performance.

Configuring SSL/TLS Termination in Nginx

To configure SSL/TLS termination, you need to set up Nginx with the necessary SSL certificates and instruct it to decrypt incoming HTTPS traffic. The steps below outline this configuration:

```
1   server {
2       listen 443 ssl;
3       server_name example.com;
4
5       ssl_certificate /etc/nginx/ssl/example.com.crt;
6       ssl_certificate_key /etc/nginx/ssl/example.com.key;
7
8       location / {
9           proxy_pass http://backend_servers;
10          proxy_set_header Host $host;
11          proxy_set_header X-Real-IP $remote_addr;
12          proxy_set_header X-Forwarded-For $proxy_add_x_forwarded_for;
13          proxy_set_header X-Forwarded-Proto $scheme;
14      }
15  }
```

This configuration sets up an Nginx server block listening on port 443 with SSL. It specifies the SSL certificate and key files. The proxy_pass directive forwards the decrypted traffic to the backend server group named 'backend_servers'. The proxy_set_header directives ensure that the backend servers receive the original client request information, crucial for logging and application functionality.

SSL/TLS Pass-Through with Nginx Stream Module

SSL/TLS pass-through can be achieved by utilizing the Nginx stream module, enabling TCP (or UDP) proxying. This method involves setting up Nginx to forward encrypted traffic to the backend without decryption. An example configuration is presented below:

```
stream {
    upstream backend_servers {
        server backend1.example.com:443;
        server backend2.example.com:443;
    }

    server {
        listen 443;
        proxy_pass backend_servers;
        ssl_preread on;
    }
}
```

In this configuration, the `stream` block defines a TCP proxy. The `upstream` directive specifies the backend servers, which are expected to decrypt the HTTPS traffic. The `ssl_preread` directive enables Nginx to read the SSL handshake to obtain the server name indicated by the client, facilitating intelligent routing decisions without decrypting the entire traffic.

Considerations

Choosing between SSL/TLS termination and pass-through depends on specific requirements for security, performance, and backend server capabilities. Termination is beneficial for offloading cryptographic tasks from the backend servers, while pass-through is preferred for maintaining end-to-end encryption. Additionally, the choice affects how session persistence and other advanced features can be configured in Nginx.

Both SSL/TLS termination and pass-through configurations offer unique advantages and require careful consideration of the trade-offs involved. By following the detailed setups outlined above, you can achieve a secure and efficient Nginx deployment that meets your application's specific needs.

5.8 Caching Content from Upstream Servers

Caching is a critical strategy in web performance optimization, and when configured properly within an Nginx reverse proxy setup, it significantly enhances content delivery speed and reduces the load on upstream servers. In essence, caching stores copies of files or dynamically generated pages for a predetermined period, ensuring that subsequent requests to the same content are served faster, directly from the cache, without the need to fetch the content again from the backend servers.

To implement caching in an Nginx reverse proxy, several directives within the server block are utilized. The primary directive to define a cache is `proxy_cache_path`, which specifies the file system path for storing cached content, along with several parameters related to cache keys, sizes, and expiration times. Following is an example of configuring the cache path:

```
1   proxy_cache_path /data/nginx/cache levels=1:2 keys_zone=my_cache:10m max_size=1g
        inactive=60m use_temp_path=off;
```

In this example, /data/nginx/cache is the location on the disk where the cache will be stored. The `levels` parameter defines the hierarchy structure of the cache directories. `keys_zone` names the cache zone (`my_cache`) and allocates 10MB of memory for storing cache keys. `max_size` specifies the maximum size of the cache on disk. `inactive` sets the duration a cached item will be kept in the cache without being accessed before it is removed.

Once the cache path is configured, the next step is to enable caching for requests. This is achieved with the `proxy_cache` directive, used within a location block where reverse proxying is configured. Here is how it is done:

```
1   location / {
2       proxy_pass http://my_upstream;
3       proxy_cache my_cache;
4       proxy_cache_valid 200 302 60m;
5       proxy_cache_valid 404 1m;
6   }
```

The `proxy_cache` directive specifies the cache zone defined earlier.

`proxy_cache_valid` directives dictate how long the response should be considered valid in the cache based on the response status code. In this configuration, successful responses (status code 200) and redirects (status code 302) are cached for 60 minutes, while 404 responses are cached for 1 minute.

Effectively managing cache requires fine-tuning based on the application's specific needs. `proxy_cache_key` allows customization of the cache key, which is crucial for ensuring the cache's effectiveness. A typical configuration might include request elements such as scheme, host, and request URI:

```
1   proxy_cache_key "$scheme$request_method$host$request_uri";
```

This configuration ensures that the cache is uniquely keyed for each combination of the request scheme (http or https), method (GET, POST, etc.), host, and the full request URI.

Additionally, for scenarios where it's essential to bypass the cache based on certain conditions, the `proxy_cache_bypass` directive is used. This can be particularly useful for ensuring that requests carrying authentication or session information are always processed by the upstream servers:

```
1   proxy_cache_bypass $http_cookie $http_authorization;
```

Here, the cache will be bypassed if either the `$http_cookie` or `$http_authorization` variables are set, effectively ensuring that authenticated user requests obtain fresh content.

Effectively caching content from upstream servers requires careful planning and configuration within your Nginx reverse proxy setup. By understanding and utilizing directives such as `proxy_cache_path`, `proxy_cache`, `proxy_cache_valid`, `proxy_cache_key`, and `proxy_cache_bypass`, it's possible to significantly enhance the performance and efficiency of content delivery, providing a better experience for end-users while reducing the load on your web infrastructure.

5.9   WebSocket Reverse Proxying

WebSocket technology enables full-duplex communication channels over a single TCP connection, making it indispensable for real-time web applications, such as gaming, chat applications, and live sports updates. When deploying WebSocket applications behind Nginx, special configuration directives are needed to properly handle the WebSocket protocol. This ensures that WebSocket connections are established and maintained through the Nginx server to the backend application servers without interruption.

To facilitate WebSocket reverse proxying, Nginx must be configured to understand the upgrade requests from the client and manage the connection upgrade process transparently. The following directives are instrumental:

```
location /wsapp {
    proxy_pass http://backend;
    proxy_http_version 1.1;
    proxy_set_header Upgrade $http_upgrade;
    proxy_set_header Connection "upgrade";
    proxy_set_header Host $host;
}
```

This configuration snippet defines a location block for the WebSocket endpoint. Let's dissect the configuration to understand its components:

- `proxy_pass http://backend;`: This directive specifies the protocol, hostname, and optional port number of the proxied server where the WebSocket request should be forwarded.

- `proxy_http_version 1.1;`: WebSocket requires HTTP/1.1 for connection upgrades. This directive ensures that Nginx uses HTTP/1.1 in its communication with the backend.

- `proxy_set_header Upgrade $http_upgrade;`: This line tells Nginx to pass along the Upgrade header from the client, which is essential for initiating protocol upgrades required by WebSocket.

127

- `proxy_set_header Connection "upgrade";`: Similarly, the Connection header needs to be set to "upgrade" to signal that the connection will transition to a different protocol.

- `proxy_set_header Host $host;`: Ensures the host header from the client request is forwarded to the backend server, which may be necessary for servers hosting multiple domains.

Performance considerations and optimizations can further enhance the WebSocket experience. Enabling the `proxy_buffers` and `proxy_read_timeout` directives can optimize buffer sizes and define read timeout values, respectively, which are critical for maintaining efficient and persistent WebSocket connections.

```
1  location /wsapp {
2      proxy_pass http://backend;
3      proxy_http_version 1.1;
4      proxy_set_header Upgrade $http_upgrade;
5      proxy_set_header Connection "upgrade";
6      proxy_set_header Host $host;
7      proxy_buffers 8 32k;
8      proxy_read_timeout 600s;
9  }
```

To verify the WebSocket reverse proxy functionality, developers can monitor the upgrade requests and responses through HTTP headers or using WebSocket client libraries and tools that provide insights into the WebSocket handshake process and subsequent data exchange.

Testing with real-world scenarios, such as reconnecting on failure and simulating varying network conditions, is essential for ensuring that the WebSocket application remains robust and responsive behind Nginx.

In summary, properly configuring Nginx for WebSocket reverse proxying ensures seamless communication between clients and WebSocket servers. The correct use of proxy directives and careful tuning of connection parameters can significantly impact the performance and reliability of WebSocket-based applications. This configuration empowers developers to leverage the full capabilities of Nginx in supporting real-time, bi-directional communication in modern web applications.

5.10 Restricting Access with Reverse Proxies

In configuring Nginx as a reverse proxy, a critical aspect to consider is securing the served applications by restricting access based on various criteria. Restricting access effectively prevents unauthorized use, safeguards sensitive information, and minimizes potential attack vectors. This section will detail different methods to restrict access using Nginx.

Blocking Access by IP Address

Nginx allows administrators to deny or allow access to their websites based on the client's IP address or range. This can be leveraged to block known malicious entities or to create a private site only accessible to specific IPs.

Below is an example on how to block access for all users except those coming from a particular IP address:

```
1   location / {
2       allow 192.168.1.100;
3       deny all;
4   }
```

In this configuration, only requests from the IP address 192.168.1.100 are allowed, while all other requests are denied.

Basic Authentication

Another common method to restrict access is through the use of basic authentication, where users are required to enter a username and password to access the application.

To implement basic authentication, you first need to create a password file using the htpasswd utility. For example, to create a file named .htpasswd:

```
1   htpasswd -c /etc/nginx/.htpasswd user1
```

Then, modify the Nginx configuration to specify the location of the password file, as shown in the below configuration:

```
1  location / {
2      auth_basic "Restricted Access";
3      auth_basic_user_file /etc/nginx/.htpasswd;
4  }
```

The directive `auth_basic` enables basic authentication, and `auth_basic_user_file` specifies the file that contains the list of allowed users and their passwords. When users attempt to access the URL, they will be prompted to enter a username and password.

Restricting Access by HTTP Referer

To prevent hotlinking, where external sites link directly to your site's resources (e.g., images or videos), and consume your bandwidth, Nginx can restrict access based on the HTTP referer header.

The following configuration demonstrates how to block access to images if the request does not come from your own domain:

```
1  location ~* \.(jpg|jpeg|png|gif)$ {
2      valid_referers none blocked ~.yourdomain.com;
3      if ($invalid_referer) {
4          return 403;
5      }
6  }
```

This setup checks the `Referer` header of the request. If the request does not come from yourdomain.com or if there is no `Referer` header, Nginx denies access by returning a 403 Forbidden status.

Implementing access restrictions via Nginx serves as a vital security measure. By understanding and utilizing these techniques, administrators can effectively control access to their web applications, reducing exposure to unauthorized users and potential threats.

5.11 Using Variables in Proxy Pass Directives

Nginx allows for a high degree of flexibility and control in the configuration of reverse proxy setups, one aspect of which includes the use
of variables in proxy_pass directives. This capability can be particularly useful in scenarios where the backend server's address might
need to be dynamically determined at runtime or when implementing more complex routing logic.

The proxy_pass directive is used to define the protocol and address
of a proxied server and the optional URI to which a location should
be mapped. Variables in Nginx can come from a variety of sources,
including built-in variables, values extracted from the request (e.g.,
headers, URIs), and those set explicitly within the configuration using the set directive.

Basic Usage

To begin using variables in proxy_pass directives, it is essential to
first understand how to define and utilize variables within the
Nginx configuration. The following is an example wherein a
variable is defined and then used in a proxy_pass directive:

```
1  location /example {
2      set $backend_server http://backend.example.com;
3      proxy_pass $backend_server;
4  }
```

In this configuration, the variable $backend_server is set to the ad-
dress of the backend server. Then, the proxy_pass directive utilizes
this variable to determine where to forward requests that match the
location block.

Dynamic Resolution

One of the strengths of using variables within proxy_pass directives
is the ability to dynamically alter the backend server selection based
on the request. This is particularly useful in environments where

131

traffic needs to be dynamically routed to different servers based on request attributes or other logic. Consider the following example:

```
1   map $request_uri $backend {
2       ~^/service1 http://service1_backend.example.com;
3       ~^/service2 http://service2_backend.example.com;
4       default http://default_backend.example.com;
5   }
6
7   server {
8       location / {
9           proxy_pass $backend;
10      }
11  }
```

In this example, a map block is used to associate different request URIs with different backend servers. The $backend variable is then dynamically set based on the request URI and used in the proxy_pass directive. This approach enables a single Nginx server to route requests to different backend servers based on the request URI pattern.

Caveats and Considerations

While using variables in proxy_pass directives offers significant flexibility, there are several important considerations:

- **Scheme Part**: When using variables, the scheme part (e.g., http or https) must be included in the variable value. Nginx requires this to correctly form the request to the backend server.

- **URI Concatenation**: If a URI specified in a proxy_pass directive does not end with a slash (/) and the proxied request URI is not passed explicitly, Nginx will concatenate the proxied request URI to the proxy_pass URI. This behavior underscores the importance of being explicit about URI handling in proxy pass configurations.

- **DNS Resolution**: Variable values in proxy_pass directives are subject to DNS resolution at the time of the request, which can introduce latency in request processing.   To minimize performance impacts, proper DNS caching should be configured.

Utilizing variables in proxy_pass directives empowers administrators with the ability to create more dynamic and responsive Nginx configurations. By understanding the basics of variable usage, as well as potential caveats, one can effectively leverage this powerful feature to achieve sophisticated reverse proxy and load balancing setups.

5.12 Troubleshooting Common Reverse Proxy and Load Balancing Issues

Troubleshooting the variety of issues that can arise with reverse proxy and load balancing configurations in Nginx requires a systematic approach. Common problems include misconfigurations, network issues, upstream server failures, and SSL/TLS related errors. By understanding these problems and their potential solutions, administrators can ensure the stability and reliability of their Nginx setups.

Upstream Server Unavailability

One prevalent issue is the unavailability of upstream servers, where Nginx cannot connect to the backend servers specified in the reverse proxy configuration. This problem often manifests as "502 Bad Gateway" or "504 Gateway Timeout" errors. To troubleshoot this issue:

- Verify the upstream servers are running and reachable from the Nginx server.

- Check the `error_log` directive's path in the Nginx configuration for specific error messages.

- Ensure the ports in the `upstream` block of Nginx configuration match the listening ports of the backend servers.

133

A snippet showcasing an example check in the Nginx configuration might look like this:

```
1  upstream backend {
2      server backend1.example.com:8080;
3      server backend2.example.com:8080;
4  }
```

Load Balancing Algorithm Misconfigurations

Incorrect configurations of load balancing algorithms could lead to uneven load distribution. For instance, configuring the round-robin method when an application requires session persistence could result in session data inconsistencies. Review the configured load balancing algorithm and the requirements of the application being served.

```
1  upstream backend {
2      least_conn;
3      server backend1.example.com;
4      server backend2.example.com;
5  }
```

The above configuration utilizes the least_conn method, which directs new connections to the server with the fewest active connections. Ensure this method aligns with the application's operational characteristics.

SSL/TLS Configuration Errors

SSL/TLS configuration errors may result in clients being unable to establish secure connections, leading to errors such as "SSL_PROTOCOL_ERROR". Key areas to verify include:

- Correctness of the SSL certificate and private key.

- Compatibility of SSL protocols and ciphers between Nginx and upstream servers.

- Proper configuration of the ssl_certificate and ssl_certificate_key directives.

An example of correctly configured SSL directives in Nginx:

```
1  server {
2      listen 443 ssl;
3      server_name example.com;
4
5      ssl_certificate /etc/nginx/ssl/example.com.crt;
6      ssl_certificate_key /etc/nginx/ssl/example.com.key;
7
8      location / {
9          proxy_pass http://backend;
10     }
11 }
```

Pooling Connections to Upstream Servers

Another critical aspect of handling reverse proxy and load balancing issues involves managing connections to upstream servers efficiently. Excessive creation and closure of connections can lead to system resource exhaustion. Using the keepalive directive in the upstream block can effectively manage persistent connections:

```
1  upstream backend {
2      server backend1.example.com;
3      server backend2.example.com;
4
5      keepalive 32;
6  }
```

This configuration allows up to 32 idle connections to be kept open for reuse, reducing the overhead associated with establishing new connections.

Troubleshooting reverse proxy and load balancing configurations in Nginx is an iterative process that demands a deep understanding of Nginx's workings, network communication principles, and the specific needs of the application being served. By methodically addressing common issues and regularly reviewing configuration settings, administrators can significantly enhance the performance, reliability, and security of their Nginx deployments.

Chapter 6

Caching Strategies in Nginx

Implementing effective caching strategies in Nginx significantly enhances web application performance by reducing server load and decreasing response times for end-users. Caching involves temporarily storing copies of files so that future requests for those files can be served faster. Nginx provides robust mechanisms for both static and dynamic content caching, allowing for granular control over what gets cached, how long it remains in the cache, and when it should be refreshed or invalidated. Mastery of caching techniques in Nginx helps in optimizing web resource delivery, improving the scalability of web services, and ensuring a smoother user experience.

6.1   Understanding the Basics of Caching

Caching in the context of Nginx refers to the process of storing a copy of files or data in a temporary storage location, known as a cache, so that future requests for these files can be served faster.

This mechanism significantly reduces the load on the server by preventing the need to repeatedly compute or fetch the same content for each request, thereby enhancing the responsiveness and performance of web applications.

To grasp the essential concepts of caching, it is pivotal to understand the distinction between static and dynamic content. Static content includes files that do not change frequently, such as images, CSS files, and JavaScript files. Dynamic content, on the other hand, is content generated on-the-fly, often personalized for individual users, like HTML pages rendered by server-side scripts.

Nginx facilitates caching for both types of content, but the methods and considerations vary. For static content, Nginx can directly cache the files, serving them rapidly without accessing the backend server. For dynamic content, Nginx uses a slightly more complex mechanism that involves caching the output of scripts and serving it for subsequent requests, which matches specific criteria.

The efficacy of caching in Nginx is governed by a set of directives that control aspects such as:

- The duration for which a file should remain in the cache, known as the cache TTL (Time To Live).

- The conditions under which a cached file should be considered stale and thereby refreshed or purged from the cache.

- The maximum size of the cache or the maximum size of individual files that can be cached.

Implementing caching requires careful planning and configuration. Overcaching can lead to serving outdated content, while undercaching can negate the performance benefits by causing excessive load on the server. Therefore, setting optimal cache parameters is crucial.

To demonstrate basic caching configuration in Nginx, consider the following snippet for static file caching:

```
1  location ~* \.(jpg|jpeg|png|gif|ico|css|js)$ {
2      expires 30d;
```

```
3     add_header Cache-Control "public";
4   }
```

In this configuration, files with the specified extensions are cached on the client's side for 30 days, indicated by the expires directive. The Cache-Control header set to "public" instructs clients and intermediaries (like proxies) that the response can be cached.

Effective caching strategies can dramatically improve the performance and scalability of web applications served by Nginx. Understanding the basics of how caching works, the types of content that can be cached, and how to control caching behavior, lays the foundation for mastering more advanced caching techniques discussed in subsequent sections of this chapter.

6.2 Types of Caching Available in Nginx

Nginx, a high-performance web server, offers a variety of caching mechanisms to optimize the delivery of web content. These mechanisms can be broadly classified into two categories: static file caching and dynamic content caching. Each type plays a crucial role in reducing server load, enhancing the speed of content delivery, and improving the overall user experience. This section delves into the specifics of these caching types and the scenarios in which they are most beneficial.

Static File Caching

Static file caching is the process of storing copies of unchanging files, such as CSS, JavaScript, and image files, so that they can be quickly served to users without being reloaded from the disk on each request. Nginx excels in this area, providing straightforward configuration options to enable efficient static file caching.

The primary directive used in Nginx for static file caching is expires. This directive allows developers to specify how long browsers should cache the static content. For instance, setting an expires directive to 30 days instructs the browser to store the static files for that duration before making another request to the server for fresh content.

```
1  location ~* \.(jpg|jpeg|png|gif|ico|css|js)$ {
2      expires 30d;
3  }
```

By serving static content directly from the cache, the server conserves resources, and end-users experience faster page load times.

Dynamic Content Caching

Dynamic content caching, on the other hand, involves temporarily storing parts of a website that do change but not on every request, such as HTML pages generated by content management systems. Unlike static content, dynamic content requires a more sophisticated approach to caching due to its potentially variable nature.

Nginx addresses dynamic content caching through its `proxy_cache` and `fastcgi_cache` directives, which are part of its reverse proxy and FastCGI modules, respectively. These modules allow Nginx to cache content from upstream servers or FastCGI processes, storing the generated content for future requests.

Configuring dynamic content caching involves setting up a cache zone and specifying cache keys, which determine how cached content is stored and retrieved. An essential aspect of dynamic caching is defining the criteria under which content is considered stale and should be refreshed.

```
1   proxy_cache_path /data/nginx/cache levels=1:2 keys_zone=my_cache:10m max_size=10
        g
2                   inactive=60m use_temp_path=off;
3
4   server {
5       location / {
6           proxy_cache my_cache;
7           proxy_pass http://my_upstream;
8           proxy_cache_key "$scheme$request_method$host$request_uri";
9           proxy_cache_valid 200 302 60m;
10          proxy_cache_use_stale error timeout updating http_500 http_502 http_503
                http_504;
11      }
12  }
```

In this configuration, `proxy_cache_path` specifies the path and parameters of the cache, including its size and duration of cached content's validity. The `proxy_cache_key` directive defines how requests are matched to cached responses, ensuring that users are served accurate and up-to-date content.

Choosing the Right Type of Caching

The choice between static and dynamic content caching in Nginx largely depends on the nature of the web application and its content. Static file caching is generally easier to implement and is suitable for assets that rarely change. Dynamic content caching, while more complex to set up, is essential for highly dynamic sites where content changes frequently but not necessarily with every request.

By effectively leveraging both types of caching, developers can significantly improve the performance and scalability of web applications, ensuring a superior experience for end-users.

In summary, Nginx provides powerful tools for both static and dynamic content caching, each catering to different types of web content. Proper configuration and understanding of these caching mechanisms are key to optimizing web application performance.

6.3 Configuring Static File Caching

Configuring static file caching in Nginx involves a straightforward process that has a profound impact on the performance and scalability of web applications. Static files, such as images, CSS, and JavaScript files, do not change frequently. By caching these files, Nginx can serve them directly from memory, significantly reducing disk I/O and speeding up response times for end users.

The primary directive involved in static file caching in Nginx is `expires`. This directive allows you to set caching headers that instruct the client's browser how long to cache the static content.

```
1   location ~* \.(jpg|jpeg|gif|png|css|js|ico|xml)$ {
2       access_log off;
3       log_not_found off;
4       expires 30d;
5   }
```

In the example above, the location block matches any requests for files with the listed extensions. The expires directive is set to 30 days (30d), telling the client's browser to cache these files for up to 30 days.

Setting access_log and log_not_found to off improves performance by reducing unnecessary logging for these static resources.

Additionally, leveraging the try_files directive can further enhance performance by minimizing processing. The try_files directive attempts to serve the requested file if it exists; otherwise, it can return a 404 error or redirect to another handler.

```
1   location / {
2       try_files $uri $uri/ =404;
3   }
```

For an effective caching strategy, it's imperative to set appropriate values for the Cache-Control and Expires headers. While the expires directive manipulates the Expires header, you can use the add_header directive to add or modify the Cache-Control header.

```
1   location ~* \.css$ {
2       expires 1y;
3       add_header Cache-Control "public, immutable";
4   }
```

This configuration sets CSS files to be cached for one year with Cache-Control directives indicating that the resource is public and immutable, signaling clients and proxies that the resource can be cached and will not change during its max-age.

To manage and modify caching behavior based on the file extension or any particular condition, the use of conditional statements within the location blocks can be employed. However, it's crucial to be cautious with conditional logic in Nginx configurations to avoid unintended side-effects.

For a high cache hit rate and efficient resource delivery, understanding and correctly implementing static file caching in Nginx is vital. Along with the proper server configuration, client-side settings play a significant role in how effective caching can be. Therefore, a comprehensive approach, considering both server and client-side configurations, yields the best performance enhancements.

6.4 Dynamic Content Caching Strategies

Dynamic content caching in Nginx demands a thoughtful approach since it involves content that can change based on user interaction or other live data. Unlike static content, which remains unchanged, dynamic content requires a mechanism that not only caches efficiently but also ensures that users receive the most current version of the content. In this section, various strategies for caching dynamic content within Nginx will be discussed.

Use of Proxy Cache

Proxy caching is a significant feature of Nginx that can be leveraged for dynamic content. It works by caching the response from a proxied server. The configuration directive for enabling proxy caching is `proxy_cache`, and it is essential to define a cache key with `proxy_cache_key` to uniquely identify cached items. An example configuration snippet is provided below:

```
1  location / {
2      proxy_pass http://backend_server;
3      proxy_cache my_cache;
4      proxy_cache_key "$scheme$proxy_host$request_uri";
5  }
```

In this example, `my_cache` refers to a cache zone defined elsewhere in the configuration. The cache key is a combination of the scheme, proxy host, and request URI, ensuring a unique entry for each request.

Cache Invalidation

Ensuring that cached dynamic content is up-to-date requires an invalidation strategy. Nginx supports cache invalidation via the proxy_cache_bypass and proxy_no_cache directives, which can be used to bypass or prevent caching based on certain conditions.

```
location / {
    proxy_pass http://backend_server;
    proxy_cache my_cache;
    proxy_cache_bypass $http_cache_control;
    proxy_no_cache $cookie_nocache $arg_nocache $http_cache_control;
}
```

In this configuration, the cache will be bypassed or not used if the $http_cache_control header from the client contains certain directives, or if $cookie_nocache or $arg_nocache variables are set, indicating that caching should not occur.

Control with HTTP Headers

HTTP headers play a pivotal role in controlling the cache behavior. The Cache-Control header in response from the backend server can instruct Nginx on how long to cache content with the proxy_cache_valid directive.

```
location / {
    proxy_pass http://backend_server;
    proxy_cache my_cache;
    proxy_cache_valid 200 302 10m;
    proxy_cache_valid 404 1m;
}
```

This configuration caches responses with 200 and 302 status codes for 10 minutes, and 404 responses for 1 minute, following the directives provided by the backend server in the Cache-Control header.

Micro-Caching

Micro-caching refers to caching dynamic content for a very short duration, often just a few seconds, to improve performance during high traffic periods without significantly affecting the content's freshness.

```
1  location / {
2      proxy_pass http://backend_server;
3      proxy_cache my_cache;
4      proxy_cache_valid 200 5s;
5  }
```

In this configuration, successful responses (200 status code) are cached for 5 seconds, providing a balance between load reduction and content freshness.

Caching dynamic content in Nginx requires careful configuration and testing to achieve the desired balance between performance and accuracy. The strategies discussed here, including proxy caching, cache invalidation, control with HTTP headers, and micro-caching, provide a framework for implementing effective dynamic content caching in Nginx.

6.5 Cache Invalidation and Purging Techniques

Cache invalidation is a critical component of the caching system in Nginx, ensuring that users receive the most up-to-date content without unnecessary delays. This process involves removing outdated or stale content from the cache, so that subsequent requests for that content are processed directly from the origin server or from an updated cache entry. There are primarily two approaches to cache invalidation in Nginx: passive expiration and active invalidation.

Passive Expiration

Passive expiration relies on predefined time-to-live (TTL) values for caching entities. When content is stored in the cache, it is assigned a TTL based on server directives or HTTP headers. Once the TTL expires, the cached content is considered stale and is removed from the cache upon the next request. Nginx checks the validity of cached content using the proxy_cache_valid directive for reverse proxy caches or `fastcgi_cache_valid` for FastCGI caches. The syntax for setting TTL is as follows:

```
1  proxy_cache_valid 200 302 10m;
2  proxy_cache_valid 404 1m;
```

In this example, responses with HTTP status codes 200 and 302 are cached for 10 minutes, while 404 responses are cached for 1 minute.

Active Invalidation

Active invalidation, in contrast, allows for immediate removal of cached content through external triggers. This approach is beneficial for content that must be updated more frequently due to changes in the underlying data or at the request of the content manager. Nginx provides the `proxy_cache_purge` directive in conjunction with third-party modules such as the ngx_cache_purge module to facilitate active invalidation. Configuring active invalidation requires modifying Nginx configuration files:

```
1  location /purge/ {
2      allow 127.0.0.1;
3      deny all;
4      proxy_cache_purge MYCACHE $scheme$http_host$request_uri;
5  }
```

With this setup, sending an HTTP request to the /purge/ path along with the desired URL to be purged actively removes the specified content from the cache. Note that MYCACHE refers to the cache zone established in the Nginx configuration.

Cache Invalidation Strategies

Choosing the right cache invalidation strategy depends on the specific requirements of the web application and the expected frequency of content updates. For static content with infrequent changes, passive expiration provides an easy-to-manage, low-overhead solution. For dynamic content or content that requires immediate updates, active invalidation is the preferred approach. It is also possible to combine both strategies for different parts of a website to optimize performance and ensure content freshness.

Best Practices

- Use cache versioning for static assets that change infrequently. By appending a version number or hash to filenames (e.g., style.v2.css), you can force the cache to treat updated files as new content without needing to purge manually.

- Set appropriate TTL values based on content update frequency and user experience requirements. Overly long TTL values may lead users to receive stale content, while excessively short TTL values can increase server load.

- Regularly monitor cache usage and performance to adjust TTL values and invalidation strategies as needed.

Implementing effective cache invalidation and purging techniques in Nginx is essential for maintaining high performance and delivering accurate, up-to-date content to end-users. By understanding and applying the principles of passive expiration and active invalidation, administrators can significantly enhance the responsiveness and efficiency of web services.

6.6 Setting Up Cache Zones

To effectively implement caching in Nginx, one must understand the concept of cache zones. A cache zone in Nginx is a designated area in memory or on disk where cache files are stored. Configuring cache zones properly is crucial for optimizing caching behavior and, ultimately, enhancing the performance of your web applications.

To define a cache zone in Nginx, the proxy_cache_path directive is used within the http block of the Nginx configuration file. This directive specifies the path to the directory where cache files will be stored, along with several important parameters that control the behavior of the cache.

Consider the following example which illustrates the basic syntax for setting up a cache zone:

```
http {
    proxy_cache_path /data/nginx/cache levels=1:2 keys_zone=my_cache:10m
                     max_size=1g inactive=1h use_temp_path=off;
}
```

In this example, several parameters are defined:

- The path /data/nginx/cache designates the directory on disk where cache files are stored.

- The levels parameter specifies the hierarchy levels of cache. In this case, "1:2" indicates a two-level directory structure.

- The keys_zone parameter names the cache zone (my_cache) and allocates memory for storing keys and metadata about cached files (in this example, 10 megabytes).

- The max_size parameter sets the maximum size of the cache. Here, it is set to 1 gigabyte.

- The inactive parameter specifies how long a file is retained in the cache without being accessed. In this example, files are removed if they have not been accessed within the last hour.

- The use_temp_path parameter, when set to off, directs Nginx to store temporary files in the same area as the cache. This can enhance performance by reducing I/O operations during caching.

Once a cache zone has been defined, it can be referenced in server blocks or location blocks to enable caching for specific requests. For instance:

```
server {
    location / {
        proxy_pass http://my_backend/;
        proxy_cache my_cache;
        proxy_cache_valid 200 302 10m;
```

```
6        proxy_cache_valid 404 1m;
7    }
8 }
```

In this server block, the `proxy_cache` directive specifies the cache zone (`my_cache`) that was defined earlier. The `proxy_cache_valid` directives control how long responses with specific status codes should be stored in the cache. Here, successful responses (HTTP status codes 200 and 302) are cached for 10 minutes, while 404 (Not Found) responses are cached for 1 minute.

It is important to note that cache zones are defined globally and can be used by multiple server blocks or locations. This allows for efficient resource utilization and simplifies the management of cache configurations across different parts of your web applications.

Setting up cache zones correctly is a fundamental step in optimizing your Nginx caching strategy. By carefully configuring cache paths, sizes, and behaviors, you can significantly improve the performance and scalability of your web services.

6.7   Controlling Cache with HTTP Headers

HTTP headers play a crucial role in controlling the behavior of cache mechanisms in Nginx. They dictate how both client-side browsers and intermediary caches handle caching of resources. Understanding and applying these headers accurately is vital for effective cache management.

Cache-Control Header

The `Cache-Control` header is fundamental in HTTP caching. It specifies directives for caching mechanisms in both requests and responses. A few common directives include:

- `no-cache` - Indicates the cached data should be revalidated with the origin server before use.

- `no-store` - Instructs caches not to store the response.

- `public` or `private` - Controls the cacheability of the response, either publicly (any cache) or privately (only by the client).

- `max-age=<seconds>` - Specifies the maximum amount of time a resource is considered fresh.

An example of setting this header in Nginx for static content would be:

```
location ~* \.(jpg|jpeg|png|gif|ico|css|js)$ {
    expires 30d;
    add_header Cache-Control "public";
}
```

This configuration sets a maximum age of 30 days for images and CSS/JS files, making them cacheable by clients and public caches.

Expires Header

The `Expires` header specifies an absolute expiration date for a resource. It is similar to the `Cache-Control: max-age` directive but uses a specific date/time instead of a duration. An effective usage of the `Expires` header can be illustrated in the configuration for caching website assets:

```
location /assets/ {
    expires 24h;
    add_header Cache-Control "public";
}
```

This configuration instructs browsers and public caches to store the assets in the specified location for 24 hours.

ETag Header

The ETag (Entity Tag) header provides a mechanism for cache revalidation. It assigns a unique identifier to each version of a resource. When a browser requests a resource it has cached, it sends the ETag value in an `If-None-Match` header. The server compares this with the current resource's ETag. If they match, it means the cached version is up-to-date, and the server returns a 304 `Not Modified` status, without resending the resource.

An Nginx configuration to enable ETag insertion is:

```
1  location / {
2      etag on;
3  }
```

Vary Header

The `Vary` header informs caches that server responses might vary based on the value of one or more request headers. This is especially important for responses that depend on headers like `Accept-Encoding` (which indicates the browser's supported compression formats). For instance, to ensure that a cache stores both compressed and uncompressed versions of a resource, you might use:

```
1  add_header Vary Accept-Encoding;
```

By correctly utilizing HTTP headers for cache control in Nginx, developers and administrators can significantly enhance the caching efficiency, leading to improved web performance and reduced server load.

6.8 Using Proxy Cache for Reverse Proxy Caching

In this section we will discuss the implementation and configuration of proxy caching in the context of Nginx operating as a reverse proxy. A reverse proxy setup is a common architectural choice for improving the performance and scalability of web applications. Nginx excels in this role, acting as an intermediary for requests from clients seeking resources from servers. By caching responses, it significantly reduces the latency and load on the application servers.

First, configuring Nginx for reverse proxy caching involves defining a cache area with the `proxy_cache_path` directive. This directive specifies the location on disk where the cache will be stored, along with several parameters that control the behavior of the cache, such as its size and the duration of cached content.

```
1   proxy_cache_path /data/nginx/cache levels=1:2 keys_zone=my_cache:10m inactive=60
      m;
```

In this example, the cache is stored in `/data/nginx/cache`, with a two-level structure for storing cache files. The `keys_zone` parameter names the cache zone (`my_cache`) and allocates 10MB of memory for storing keys and metadata. Cached content that has not been accessed within the last 60 minutes (`inactive=60m`) will be removed from the cache.

Next, the `proxy_cache` directive is used within a server or location block to enable caching for requests handled by the block. The value of this directive must match the name of a cache zone defined by a `proxy_cache_path` directive.

```
1   location / {
2       proxy_pass http://my_backend/;
3       proxy_cache my_cache;
4   }
```

This configuration enables caching for requests to the location block, using the `my_cache` zone. Requests are passed to a backend server group defined by the `proxy_pass` directive.

Controlling the duration for which content is cached is achieved with the `proxy_cache_valid` directive. This directive specifies how long responses with particular status codes should be stored in the cache.

```
1   proxy_cache_valid 200 302 10m;
2   proxy_cache_valid 404 1m;
```

Here, successful responses (200) and redirects (302) are cached for 10 minutes, while 404 (Not Found) responses are only cached for 1 minute.

For fine-grained control over caching, it's often necessary to manipulate HTTP headers. The `proxy_cache_bypass` directive causes Nginx to bypass the cache for requests with headers matching specified conditions, while the `proxy_no_cache` directive prevents responses from being cached if they have headers matching specified conditions.

```
1  proxy_cache_bypass $cookie_nocache $arg_nocache;
2  proxy_no_cache $cookie_nocache $arg_nocache;
```

In this configuration, if a request contains a nocache cookie or query parameter, Nginx will bypass the cache for serving the request and also avoid caching the response.

Monitoring and debugging the behavior of the proxy cache can be facilitated by including the $upstream_cache_status variable in the access log format. This variable indicates whether a response was served from the cache (HIT), fetched from the backend and cached (MISS), bypassed (BYPASS), or served from the cache but marked to be refreshed (STALE).

```
cache status: HIT
```

Configuring Nginx as a reverse proxy with caching capabilities can significantly improve the responsiveness and scalability of web applications. By carefully specifying cache storage, controlling cache duration, and manipulating cache behavior through HTTP headers, developers can optimize application performance and ensure a smooth user experience.

6.9 Micro-Caching for Dynamic Content

Micro-caching is a term widely used in web technologies to refer to the caching of dynamically generated content for a very short period, typically from one to a few seconds. This approach is particularly useful for improving the performance of highly dynamic sites where content changes frequently but still can be served from cache to multiple users within its short lifespan. Nginx, through its proxy caching capabilities, offers straightforward mechanisms to implement micro-caching, which can significantly reduce the load on web applications by limiting repeated database queries and computations for the same content requested within the caching window.

To initiate micro-caching for dynamic content in Nginx, one must first configure a cache zone. This process involves specifying a location in the file system where cached content will be stored and setting parameters that determine the cache's behavior. Consider the following configuration in the `http` block of your Nginx configuration file:

```
1  http {
2      proxy_cache_path /data/nginx/cache levels=1:2 keys_zone=microcache:5m
             max_size=1000m
3                          inactive=60m use_temp_path=off;
4  }
```

In this example, `proxy_cache_path` defines the path to the cache storage directory and various parameters for the cache, such as the structure of the cache keys directory (`levels=1:2`), the name and size of the cache zone (`keys_zone=microcache:5m`), the maximum size of the cache (`max_size=1000m`), and the duration for which content remains in the cache without being accessed before it is considered inactive and potentially deleted (`inactive=60m`).

With the cache zone configured, the next step is to apply micro-caching to specific locations or server blocks. This is done by indicating when and how to cache responses and for how long. Below is an example of a server block configuration that utilizes the microcache zone for caching dynamic content:

```
1  server {
2      location / {
3          proxy_pass http://backend;
4          proxy_set_header Host $host;
5          proxy_cache microcache;
6          proxy_cache_valid 200 1s;
7          proxy_cache_use_stale updating;
8      }
9  }
```

Here, `proxy_cache` specifies the cache zone to use. The directive `proxy_cache_valid 200 1s` instructs Nginx to cache responses with a 200 (OK) HTTP status code for 1 second. This is the essence of micro-caching: storing the response of dynamic content for a brief period. The `proxy_cache_use_stale` updating line allows Nginx to serve a stale response from cache for concurrent requests while a new version of the cached content is being generated in the background, enhancing the user experience by reducing wait times.

An important benefit of micro-caching is its ability to significantly reduce the load on the backend server. Even caching dynamic content for just one second can alleviate the impact of hundreds or thousands of simultaneous requests to dynamic pages, resulting in smoother web application performance and a better user experience.

In the context of monitoring and tuning the performance of micro-caching, it is essential to analyze the hit ratio of the cache. A cache hit occurs when a request is served from the cache, while a miss indicates that the content needed to be fetched from the backend and potentially cached for subsequent requests. Monitoring tools and Nginx's own logging capabilities can provide insights into cache performance, enabling further optimization.

```
cache hit (total): 90%
cache miss (total): 10%
```

This example output shows a high cache hit ratio, indicating that a significant portion of requests for dynamic content is being served from the cache, evidencing the effectiveness of micro-caching in reducing server load and improving response times.

In summary, micro-caching for dynamic content is a powerful strategy in Nginx for managing the performance of web applications that feature frequently changing data. It requires careful configuration and monitoring but can lead to substantial improvements in server efficiency and user experience.

6.10   Integrating Third-Party Caching Tools with Nginx

Integrating third-party caching tools with Nginx allows leveraging external caching mechanisms to further enhance web performance and reduce server load. This can be particularly beneficial in complex environments where advanced caching logic or distributed caching systems are needed. In this section, we will explore several popular third-party caching solutions and how they can be integrated with Nginx.

Varnish is a widely used HTTP accelerator designed for content-heavy dynamic web sites. To integrate Varnish with Nginx, Varnish is placed in front of Nginx. This setup implies that client requests hit Varnish first, where cached content is served directly, if available. If not, Varnish passes the request to Nginx. This can be achieved by configuring Varnish to listen on port 80 and setting Nginx to listen on a different port, such as 8080, ensuring that external traffic does not directly reach Nginx.

```
1   # Example Varnish configuration to forward requests to Nginx
2   backend default {
3       .host = "localhost";
4       .port = "8080";
5   }
6
7   # Nginx listens on port 8080 for requests forwarded by Varnish
8   server {
9       listen 8080;
10      server_name mywebsite.com;
11
12      location / {
13          # Nginx configuration details
14      }
15  }
```

Redis can also be integrated with Nginx for caching through the use of the ngx_http_redis module. This setup is beneficial for dynamic content caching where Nginx directly queries Redis for cached content before processing the request further.   Configuration involves setting up the Redis server and modifying Nginx configuration to use Redis for caching certain requests.

```
1    # Example Nginx configuration to use Redis for caching
2    location /cache/ {
3        set $redis_key $uri;
4        redis_pass redis-server:6379;
5        error_page 404 = @fallback;
6    }
7
8    location @fallback {
9        proxy_pass http://backend;
10   }
```

Memcached, another popular caching solution, can be integrated similarly to Redis. The ngx_http_memcached_module allows Nginx to retrieve cached content from Memcached. This is particularly useful for storing HTML fragments or page elements that can be directly served by Nginx, reducing the need to generate dynamic content on every request.

```
1    # Example Nginx configuration to use Memcached for caching
2    location / {
3        set $memcached_key $uri;
4        memcached_pass memcached-host:11211;
5        default_type text/html;
6        error_page 404 502 = @backend;
7    }
8
9    location @backend {
10       proxy_pass http://backend-server;
11   }
```

In addition to the above, integrating third-party caching tools with Nginx might require adjusting cache headers and understanding the caching logic specific to each tool. Deployment considerations, such as network latency between Nginx and the caching tool, and cache invalidation strategies, must also be accounted for to ensure an efficient caching solution.

6.11 Caching Best Practices

Caching, an essential aspect of web service optimization, requires adherence to a set of best practices to achieve its maximum potential. These practices revolve around ensuring cache efficiency, the freshness of content, and sensible resource management. Implementing these can substantially decrease load times and enhance user experience, while also reducing server load.

- **Selective Caching:** Not all content benefits equally from being cached. Static assets, such as images, CSS, and JavaScript files, are ideal candidates due to their infrequent updates. Dynamic content, particularly that which is user-specific or rapidly changing, requires a more cautious approach. Use Nginx's `location` directive to specify paths for caching and apply different caching rules based on content type or request method.

- **Cache Duration:** Setting an optimal cache duration (`expires` directive in Nginx) is critical. While longer durations reduce the number of requests to the origin server, they can serve stale content to users. A general rule is to assign longer durations to assets that change infrequently and shorter for more dynamic content. Employing a versioning strategy for static assets (e.g., appending a version number to filenames) can ensure that users receive the most current files without compromising caching efficiency.

- **Cache Invalidation:** Proper invalidation mechanics are vital to maintaining cache effectiveness. Nginx allows for manual invalidation through configuration changes but lacks direct commands for cache purging. Instead, one must rely on external tools or scripts to clear cache files from disk or use proxy cache directives combined with cache keys to control cache versions.

- **Using Cache Headers:** Proper utilization of HTTP cache headers can augment Nginx caching strategies significantly. Headers such as `Cache-Control`, `Expires`, and `ETag` can dictate how and when caches are stored and validated.1 For dynamic content, leveraging `Cache-Control` headers to designate content as non-cacheable or to specify maximum age can guide both browser and proxy caches.

- **Cache Zone Configuration:** Allocating sufficient memory for cache zones (`proxy_cache_path` directive) ensures that Nginx can store a practical cache size. Monitor usage and hit rates to adjust the size appropriately. Too small a cache zone leads to frequent cache evictions, while an excessively large cache may underutilize resources.

- **Monitoring and Logging:** Establishing mechanisms for monitoring cache status and performance is crucial. Nginx offers access and error logs, which can be configured to record cache hits and misses. These logs, along with custom monitoring tools, can be instrumental in diagnosing issues and optimizing cache configurations.

- **Security Considerations:** Ensure that cached content does not expose sensitive information. Utilize Nginx directives to avoid caching pages that may contain user-specific data, employ secure connections (HTTPS) for cached content, and consider the use of cache control headers to prevent sensitive data from being stored in public caches.

It's important to strike a balance between caching efficiency and content freshness. Employing a robust caching strategy involves not only configuring Nginx appropriately but also adapting the website's content and server architecture to make optimal use of caching capabilities. Continual monitoring and adjustment based on analytics and usage patterns are necessary to maintain an effective cache strategy over time.

6.12 Monitoring and Debugging Cache Performance

Monitoring and debugging cache performance in Nginx is essential for maintaining optimal web application responsiveness and ensuring that caching strategies are effectively contributing to the reduction of server load and improvement of end-user experience. This section elaborates on the tools and techniques available for this purpose, focusing on practical approaches to identify and resolve caching issues.

Accessing Cache Logs

Nginx logs provide valuable insights into the operation of the cache. To effectively monitor cache performance, it is important to configure logging specifically for cache events. This can be achieved by modifying the Nginx configuration file, typically found at /etc/nginx/nginx.conf, to include custom log formats that capture cache status information.

The following is an example configuration that adds a custom log format named cache_log which includes the cache status ($upstream_cache_status):

```
 1   http {
 2       log_format cache_log '$remote_addr - $upstream_cache_status
 3                            [$time_local] "$request" '
 4                            '$status $body_bytes_sent "$http_referer" '
 5                            '"$http_user_agent"';
 6
 7       server {
 8           access_log /var/log/nginx/cache_access.log cache_log;
 9           ...
10       }
11   }
```

The $upstream_cache_status variable indicates whether a response was served from cache (HIT), missed the cache (MISS), or bypassed the cache (BYPASS). Logging this information is crucial for understanding cache behavior and identifying patterns that may suggest misconfigurations or opportunities for optimization.

Analyzing Cache Logs

Analysis of cache logs can be performed using standard text-processing tools such as grep, awk, or more sophisticated log analysis software. The objective is to quantify cache hits versus misses and identify anomalies such as unusually high cache miss rates which could indicate a problem.

A simple analysis can be performed by counting occurrences of cache hits and misses using the following grep commands:

```
 1   grep 'HIT' /var/log/nginx/cache_access.log | wc -l
```

```
2   grep 'MISS' /var/log/nginx/cache_access.log | wc -l
```

These commands calculate the number of lines in the cache access log that contain the phrases 'HIT' and 'MISS', respectively, providing a quick overview of cache effectiveness.

Using Nginx Cache Status Module

The Nginx cache status module, when enabled, provides a real-time view of cache performance metrics via a designated status page. This module must be explicitly included during the Nginx installation process with the --with-http_stub_status_module configuration flag.

To activate the cache status page, add the following configuration inside an appropriate server block in the Nginx configuration file:

```
1   server {
2       location /nginx_status {
3           stub_status on;
4           allow 127.0.0.1; # Only allow access from localhost
5           deny all; # Deny access from all other IPs
6       }
7   }
```

Accessing this page from a web browser or using tools like curl will display cache metrics such as active connections, handled requests, and reading/writing/waiting statuses. These metrics are invaluable for diagnosing performance bottlenecks and ensuring that the cache is functioning as intended.

Debugging Caching Issues

When cache performance issues are identified, a systematic approach to debugging is required. This involves verifying cache configuration settings, ensuring that cache keys are correctly specified, and validating that the content intended to be cached is not inadvertently excluded by cache bypass conditions.

Additionally, leveraging the debug_log directive in Nginx can provide detailed information about the cache decision process for individual requests. This directive should be used judiciously, as it can generate large volumes of logs and potentially impact performance.

In summary, diligent monitoring and debugging of cache performance are crucial for maximizing the efficiency of Nginx caching strategies. By employing the methods outlined above, administrators and developers can gain deep insights into cache behavior, allowing for targeted optimizations and improved web application delivery.

Chapter 7

Securing Nginx: Security Best Practices and Modules

Securing Nginx involves implementing a set of best practices and leveraging specific modules designed to enhance the security of web services. This includes securing the Nginx server from common web vulnerabilities, configuring SSL/TLS for encrypted connections, and applying various security headers to mitigate attacks. Nginx also supports rate limiting and access control mechanisms to prevent abuse. Through careful configuration and the adoption of security-focused modules, administrators can safeguard their web applications against a wide range of threats, ensuring the integrity, confidentiality, and availability of hosted services and data.

7.1   Overview of Web Security and Nginx

Web security constitutes a fundamental aspect of internet operations, with the objective of safeguarding data from unauthorized access, alteration, or destruction. It encompasses measures taken to protect web applications and services against a spectrum of threats and attacks such as SQL injection, Cross-Site Scripting (XSS), Denial of Service (DoS), and many others. Effective web security not only protects confidential data but also ensures the availability and integrity of web services.

Nginx, originally designed as a web server for high concurrency, performance, and low memory usage, has evolved into a versatile server capable of functioning as a reverse proxy, load balancer, HTTP cache, and web server. Its lightweight and modular architecture makes it ideally suited for securing web applications. Nginx's ability to efficiently handle and manage thousands of simultaneous connections makes it a key component in building secure and scalable web infrastructures.

To integrate security into Nginx operations, several practices and modules have been developed. These are designed to configure the server in a manner that maximizes its security capabilities while minimizing potential vulnerabilities. Some of the core practices include:

- Tightening file system permissions to limit access to critical files and directories.

- Configuring SSL/TLS to encrypt data in transit between the server and clients.

- Implementing HTTP security headers to protect against common web vulnerabilities.

- Using authentication mechanisms to restrict access to web resources.

- Applying rate limiting and access control to prevent abuse and mitigate DoS attacks.

- Regularly updating and patching Nginx to address known security vulnerabilities.

Nginx supports a range of modules that enhance its security capabilities. These include:

- `ngx_http_ssl_module`: Enables SSL/TLS support to secure connections.

- `ngx_http_auth_basic_module`: Provides basic authentication for restricting access.

- `ngx_http_access_module`: Allows or denies access based on IP address.

- `ngx_http_limit_req_module` and `ngx_http_limit_conn_module`: Implement rate limiting to control request volume and connection concurrency.

Leveraging these features and modules requires a careful approach to configuration. The following demonstrates a simple example of enabling SSL in Nginx:

```
1  server {
2      listen 443 ssl;
3      server_name example.com;
4
5      ssl_certificate /etc/nginx/ssl/example.com.crt;
6      ssl_certificate_key /etc/nginx/ssl/example.com.key;
7
8      ssl_protocols TLSv1.2 TLSv1.3;
9      ssl_ciphers HIGH:!aNULL:!MD5;
10
11     # Additional SSL configuration...
12 }
```

Upon successfully implementing the SSL configuration, the server's response to secure requests can be verified as follows:

```
$ curl -I https://example.com
HTTP/2 200
server: nginx/1.18.0
date: Mon, 01 Jan 2023 12:00:00 GMT
content-type: text/html
```

```
content-length: 612
last-modified: Mon, 01 Jan 2023 12:00:00 GMT
...
```

Nginx plays a pivotal role in securing web applications through its scalable architecture and support for a wide array of security measures.   By implementing best practices and leveraging appropriate modules, web administrators can significantly enhance the security posture of their web services.

7.2   Securing Nginx Installation and File Permissions

Securing the Nginx installation and configuring appropriate file permissions are fundamental steps towards hardening the web server against unauthorized access and potential security threats. This process involves setting correct ownership and permissions for files and directories, minimizing the risk of malicious exploitation.

To begin, it is important to ensure that Nginx runs under a non-privileged, dedicated user and group. This practice limits the possible damage in the event of a compromise, as the attacker would have access only to the permissions granted to the Nginx user, rather than to the entire system. The default configuration typically sets Nginx to run under the 'nginx' user and group, but this can be verified and adjusted as necessary in the Nginx configuration file, usually located at /etc/nginx/nginx.conf. The pertinent configuration directive resembles:

```
1  user nginx;
```

Adjusting file and directory permissions is next. Critical Nginx files, such as configuration files, should be readable by the Nginx user but not writable. Likewise, access to these files should be tightly controlled, restricting them to only the necessary users and groups. As a best practice, the root directory, configuration files, and any server content should belong to the root user and the Nginx group, with permissions set accordingly. For instance, the Nginx configuration directory and its files can be secured with:

```
1   sudo chown -R root:nginx /etc/nginx
2   sudo chmod 750 /etc/nginx
3   sudo chmod 640 /etc/nginx/nginx.conf
```

These commands change the ownership of the /etc/nginx directory and its contents to the root user and Nginx group, then set the directory permissions to 750 (read, write, and execute for the owner; read and execute for the group; no permissions for others) and the main Nginx configuration file permissions to 640 (read and write for the owner; read for the group; no permissions for others).

Limiting access to the Nginx server's document root, which contains the web content served to clients, is equally important. The document root should not be writable by the Nginx process; instead, it should be readable to ensure the webserver can serve content without unnecessary write access, which could be exploited by attackers to alter web content or perform other malicious activities. Permissions can be adjusted with:

```
1   sudo chown -R root:nginx /var/www/html
2   sudo chmod 755 /var/www/html
```

This command sets the ownership of the document root to the root user and Nginx group and adjusts permissions to 755 (read, write, and execute for the owner; read and execute for the group and others), ensuring that the content is readable and served by Nginx without granting undue permissions.

Lastly, for enhanced security, it is advisable to regularly review file and directory permissions as part of the server's routine maintenance. Scripts or automated tools can aid in monitoring permissions, ensuring that any deviations from the intended configurations are promptly identified and rectified.

Securing the Nginx installation by properly configuring file and directory permissions is a crucial step in protecting the web server environment. By adhering to the principle of least privilege and regularly reviewing system permissions, administrators can significantly reduce the server's attack surface, thereby strengthening its security posture against potential threats.

7.3   Using SSL/TLS for Secure Connections

Ensuring encrypted connections between the Nginx server and clients is vital for maintaining the confidentiality and integrity of the data in transit. SSL (Secure Sockets Layer) and TLS (Transport Layer Security) protocols are the cornerstones for securing communications on the internet. TLS, the successor to SSL, provides stronger encryption algorithms and better security protocols. For simplicity, the term SSL will be used interchangeably with TLS in this section, though TLS is recommended for all new deployments.

To begin, it's important to understand the process of configuring SSL/TLS for Nginx. This involves obtaining a certificate, configuring Nginx to use that certificate, and then fine-tuning the SSL settings to enhance security.

- **Obtaining an SSL/TLS Certificate**: There are several ways to obtain an SSL/TLS certificate. The most common method is via a Certificate Authority (CA), such as Let's Encrypt, which provides free certificates. Alternatively, certificates can be purchased from commercial CAs.

- **Configuring Nginx to Use SSL/TLS**: After acquiring a certificate, it must be configured for use with Nginx. This involves modifying the Nginx configuration files to include the SSL certificate and the private key.

- **Enhancing SSL Configuration**: To maximize the security of SSL/TLS connections, various SSL settings should be adjusted. This includes configuring strong ciphers, enabling HSTS (HTTP Strict Transport Security), and disabling old and vulnerable versions of the protocol.

To configure Nginx to use an SSL certificate, the server block in the Nginx configuration file needs to be adjusted. Below is an example configuration:

```
1   server {
2      listen 443 ssl;
3      server_name example.com;
4
5      ssl_certificate /etc/nginx/ssl/example.com.crt;
6      ssl_certificate_key /etc/nginx/ssl/example.com.key;
7
8      ssl_session_cache shared:SSL:10m;
9      ssl_session_timeout 10m;
10
11     ssl_ciphers 'ECDHE-RSA-AES128-GCM-SHA256:ECDHE-ECDSA-AES128-GCM-SHA256:ECDHE-
           RSA-AES256-GCM-SHA384:ECDHE-ECDSA-AES256-GCM-SHA384:DHE-RSA-AES128-GCM-
           SHA256:DHE-DSS-AES128-GCM-SHA256:kEDH+AESGCM:ECDHE-RSA-AES128-SHA256:
           ECDHE-ECDSA-AES128-SHA256:ECDHE-RSA-AES128-SHA:ECDHE-ECDSA-AES128-SHA:
           ECDHE-RSA-AES256-SHA384:ECDHE-ECDSA-AES256-SHA384:ECDHE-RSA-AES256-SHA:
           ECDHE-ECDSA-AES256-SHA:DHE-RSA-AES128-SHA256:DHE-RSA-AES128-SHA:DHE-DSS-
           AES128-SHA256:DHE-RSA-AES256-SHA256:DHE-DSS-AES256-SHA:DHE-RSA-AES256-
           SHA:AES128-GCM-SHA256:AES256-GCM-SHA384:AES128-SHA256:AES256-SHA256:
           AES128-SHA:AES256-SHA:AES:CAMELLIA:DES-CBC3-SHA:!aNULL:!eNULL:!EXPORT:!
           DES:!RC4:!MD5:!PSK:!aECDH:!EDH-DSS-DES-CBC3-SHA:!EDH-RSA-DES-CBC3-SHA:!
           KRB5-DES-CBC3-SHA';
12     ssl_prefer_server_ciphers on;
13
14     ...
15  }
```

This configuration enables SSL for the server block, specifies the location of the SSL certificate and key, and sets various parameters to optimize and secure SSL/TLS connections.

Furthermore, it is recommended to regularly test the SSL/TLS configuration using tools like SSL Labs' SSL Test to ensure that the server is configured with strong ciphers and protocols, and is not vulnerable to common SSL/TLS attacks and weaknesses.

Configuring SSL/TLS for Nginx is not only about enabling encrypted connections but also about ensuring that those connections are as secure as possible. This involves obtaining a proper certificate, configuring Nginx correctly, and continuously monitoring and tweaking the SSL/TLS settings as necessary. By doing so, administrators can significantly enhance the security of the data in transit, protecting both their users and their web applications from eavesdropping and data breaches.

7.4   Implementing HTTP Security Headers

Implementing HTTP security headers is a crucial step in safeguarding an Nginx server and the web applications it hosts. These headers
instruct the browser on how to behave when handling the site's content, thereby mitigating a variety of web-based vulnerabilities and
attacks. This section elucidates on the key HTTP security headers,
their purpose, and how to configure them in Nginx.

Content Security Policy (CSP)

The Content Security Policy (CSP) header reduces the risk of cross-
site scripting (XSS) attacks by declaring which dynamic resources are
allowed to load. A strict CSP can effectively prevent the execution
of unauthorized scripts by specifying allowable sources for scripts,
styles, and other resources.

```
1   add_header Content-Security-Policy "default-src 'self'; script-src 'self' https
        ://apis.example.com";
```

In the example above, 'default-src 'self'' restricts all content to the
originating site, and 'script-src 'self' https://apis.example.com'
allows scripts to be loaded from the site itself and a designated
external source, enhancing the site's resistance to XSS attacks.

X-Content-Type-Options

The X-Content-Type-Options header stops the browser from trying
to mime-sniff the content-type of a response away from the one declared by the server. This prevents attacks where an uploaded file
with a malicious script is executed because of incorrect MIME type
detection.

```
1   add_header X-Content-Type-Options "nosniff";
```

By including this header with the value 'nosniff', administrators
ensure that browsers use the content type declared in the

'Content-Type' header without attempting to guess the MIME type, thereby neutralizing this attack vector.

X-Frame-Options

X-Frame-Options controls if a browser should allow a page to be framed or embedded in an iframe, object, embed, or applet. This header can mitigate clickjacking attacks, where an attacker deceives a user into clicking on something different from what the user perceives.

```
1  add_header X-Frame-Options "SAMEORIGIN";
```

The value 'SAMEORIGIN' allows framing only by pages with the same origin as the page itself. This setting restricts attackers' ability to embed the page in a frame on a malicious site, significantly reducing the risk of clickjacking attacks.

Strict-Transport-Security

The HTTP Strict-Transport-Security (HSTS) header forces the browser to use HTTPS for communication instead of HTTP, thereby securing all data exchanges between the client and the server.

```
1  add_header Strict-Transport-Security "max-age=31536000; includeSubDomains";
```

This header, with a 'max-age' directive indicating the duration (in seconds) for which the browser should only use HTTPS, and an optional 'includeSubDomains' directive enforcing the policy for all subdomains, is effective against man-in-the-middle attacks.

Summary of Implementation

To implement these security headers, the configuration directives provided above can be added to the relevant server blocks in Nginx's configuration file ('nginx.conf' or any specific site configuration files). It's important to test the configuration for any potential issues by reloading Nginx and checking the site's functionality and header delivery using tools like browser developer consoles or online header checking services.

Next steps entail the continuous monitoring and tweaking of configured headers based on evolving web standards and emerging security threats, ensuring that the web application's security posture remains robust and responsive to the ever-changing landscape of web vulnerabilities.

7.5 Limiting   Access   with   Basic Authentication

Basic Authentication, as facilitated by Nginx, is a method of restricting access to certain parts of a website by requiring users to input a username and a password. This practice is invaluable in protecting sensitive areas of a site or application, such as administrative interfaces or private directories. It operates by sending a prompt to the user's browser, which requires the input of valid credentials to proceed. If the provided username and password match those on the server, access is granted. If not, access is denied.

To implement Basic Authentication in Nginx, one must first create a password file using the htpasswd utility, which comes with the Apache package. This file will store the usernames and encrypted passwords. If htpasswd is not already installed, it can typically be installed through your operating system's package manager.

The command to create a new password file and add a user is as follows:

```
1   htpasswd -c /etc/nginx/.htpasswd user1
```

In this command, -c specifies the creation of a new file, /etc/nginx/.htpasswd is the path where the password file will be stored, and user1 is the username for which a password is being created. The command will prompt for a password, which will be encrypted and stored in the specified file.

Once the password file has been created, the next step is to configure
Nginx to use this file for authenticating users. This is done by editing
the Nginx configuration file for the site or application requiring protection. The necessary directives are added within a location block,
indicating the protected area:

```
1  location /protected/ {
2      auth_basic "Restricted Access";
3      auth_basic_user_file /etc/nginx/.htpasswd;
4  }
```

In this configuration, the `location` directive specifies the path to be
protected. `auth_basic` enables Basic Authentication and sets the
message that will be displayed in the authentication prompt.
`auth_basic_user_file` points to the file containing the encrypted
credentials. Requests to `/protected/` will now prompt the user to
log in.

It's important to note that Basic Authentication sends credentials in
a format that is easily decoded. As such, it should always be used in
conjunction with SSL/TLS, ensuring that the login information is
encrypted during transmission. To enforce this, the `ssl` directive
should be enabled, and a valid certificate should be configured for
the server.

Basic Authentication is a straightforward but effective measure for
limiting access on a web server. However, for added security,
consider combining it with other restrictions, such as IP-based
access control or implementing more advanced authentication
mechanisms provided by third-party modules.

By properly implementing Basic Authentication, administrators can
significantly enhance the security posture of their Nginx server, effectively safeguarding sensitive areas from unauthorized access.

7.6   Securing Against Brute Force Attacks

Brute force attacks are a common threat to web servers, attempting
unauthorized access by systematically checking all possible
passwords until the correct one is found. To defend Nginx servers

against brute force attacks, several strategies and modules can be implemented for enhanced security.

Rate Limiting

One effective measure is to introduce rate limiting on authentication attempts. The `limit_req` module allows administrators to specify a maximum number of requests that can be processed within a given time frame from a single IP address.

```
1  limit_req_zone $binary_remote_addr zone=mylimit:10m rate=5r/m;
2  server {
3      location /login {
4          limit_req zone=mylimit burst=5 nodelay;
5      }
6  }
```

In the above configuration, the `limit_req_zone` directive sets up a shared memory zone named `mylimit`, allocated with 10 megabytes of memory to track the incoming IP addresses and their request rates. The rate is defined as 5 requests per minute ($5r/m$). The `limit_req` directive applies this rate limiting to the `/login` endpoint, with a burst capability of 5 requests, allowing for a slight excess over the rate limit without immediate rejection.

Fail2Ban Integration

For more sophisticated protection, integrating Fail2Ban with Nginx can effectively block IP addresses that exhibit malicious patterns, including repeated failed login attempts. Fail2Ban monitors log files for specific error patterns and bans IPs that exceed a defined threshold by updating firewall rules.

To configure Fail2Ban with Nginx, create a filter in `/etc/fail2ban/filter.d/nginx-login.conf`:

```
1  [Definition]
2  failregex = ^<HOST> -.*POST /login HTTP/1.1" 401
3  ignoreregex =
```

This regex pattern identifies failed login attempts by looking for

HTTP 401 unauthorized response codes in the Nginx access logs. Next, define a jail in /etc/fail2ban/jail.local:

```
1  [nginx-login]
2  enabled = true
3  filter = nginx-login
4  logpath = /var/log/nginx/access.log
5  maxretry = 5
6  findtime = 300
7  bantime = 600
```

The maxretry option sets the threshold for failed attempts at 5 within the findtime of 300 seconds (5 minutes), resulting in a bantime of 600 seconds (10 minutes) where the offending IP is banned from making further requests.

Password Policies

Strengthening password policies is another crucial step in thwarting brute force attacks. Requiring complex passwords that include a mix of letters, numbers, and special characters reduces the likelihood of passwords being easily guessed. Enforce these policies through the application layer and educate users on the importance of strong passwords.

Implementing these measures significantly enhances the security posture of Nginx against brute force attacks, ensuring the server and its hosted applications remain protected.

7.7 Protection Against Web Application Vulnerabilities

In addressing the protection against web application vulnerabilities, an essential aspect is understanding the common types of vulnerabilities that Nginx and associated web applications may face. These vulnerabilities include but are not limited to Cross-Site Scripting (XSS), SQL Injection, Cross-Site Request Forgery (CSRF), and File Inclusion vulnerabilities. An effective strategy comprises both preventive measures and reactive measures to mitigate these risks.

Cross-Site Scripting (XSS)

XSS vulnerabilities allow attackers to inject malicious scripts into web pages viewed by other users. To prevent XSS attacks in Nginx, one should employ Content Security Policy (CSP) headers. The CSP header instructs the browser to only execute or render resources from the website's domain, thereby preventing the execution of malicious scripts from external sources.

```
1   add_header Content-Security-Policy "default-src 'self'; script-src 'self' https
        ://apis.example.com";
```

This directive ensures that all resources in a web page are loaded from the domain itself ('self'), except for scripts from a trusted domain ('https://apis.example.com').

SQL Injection

SQL Injection attacks involve insertion or "injection" of a SQL query via the input data from the client to the application. A robust method to mitigate such attacks is to leverage the Nginx 'ngx_http_limit_req_module' module to limit the rate of requests a client can make to the server, reducing the speed and efficacy of automated injection tools.

```
1   limit_req_zone $binary_remote_addr zone=mylimit:10m rate=10r/m;
2   server {
3       location /login {
4           limit_req zone=mylimit burst=5 nodelay;
5       }
6   }
```

This configuration limits the request rate to 10 requests per minute with a burst capability of 5 additional requests, significantly mitigating brute-force SQL injection attempts.

Cross-Site Request Forgery (CSRF)

CSRF attacks trick a user into executing unwanted actions on a web application in which they are authenticated. Mitigation involves the application of anti-CSRF tokens in web applications and using Nginx to validate these tokens.

File Inclusion Vulnerabilities

File inclusion vulnerabilities allow an attacker to include files on a server through the web application. This can lead to remote code execution. To protect against such vulnerabilities, one critical step is to ensure that user-supplied input is not used directly in file include statements and to implement strict input validation.

Additionally, Nginx configurations can be tightened to restrict executable permissions and to limit direct access to sensitive files.

```
1  location ~* \.(php|jsp|asp|sh|cgi)$ {
2      return 403;
3  }
4
5  location /uploads/ {
6      location ~* \.(php|php5|php7)$ {
7          return 403;
8      }
9  }
```

This configuration blocks direct access to executable files in the entire server and specifically in the '/uploads/' directory, providing an additional layer of protection against file inclusion attacks.

Safeguarding web applications hosted on Nginx from common vulnerabilities involves a multifaceted approach including configuring security headers, restraining access with rate limiting and access control, and leveraging Nginx modules designed for security. Regular audits, updates, and adopting security best practices further fortify the application's defenses against emerging and evolving web application threats.

177

7.8   Configuring Nginx Firewalls

Configuring firewalls within Nginx entails the application of certain rules and directives to regulate traffic flow to and from the server. This involves the utilization of module features and server block configurations to effectively mitigate potential threats.   It's paramount to recognize that firewall configurations act as a primary line of defense against unauthorized access and various web-based attacks.

Understanding the Basics of Nginx as a Firewall

Nginx, by its design, can be utilized as a robust and efficient firewall due to its ability to manage and control both inbound and outbound traffic using specific directives. This capability facilitates a protective barrier around web applications, guarding them against unwarranted intrusions and ensuring that only legitimate traffic is allowed.

Employing Nginx to Block Unwanted Traffic

To block unwanted traffic effectively, Nginx administrators can employ an array of methods, including IP blocking, user agent restrictions, and the implementation of rate limiting. These methods can be configured within the Nginx server blocks or within the global http block to enforce broad or specific traffic rules.

IP Blocking

IP blocking is a fundamental method used to deny access from specific IP addresses or ranges that are known to be malicious or unnecessary for the operation of the web services hosted.

```
1  server {
2    location / {
3        deny 192.168.1.1;
4        allow all;
```

```
5        }
6    }
```

This snippet shows a basic configuration where access from the IP address 192.168.1.1 is explicitly denied. All other IP addresses are permitted access by the 'allow all' directive.

Blocking Access Based on User Agent

Some attacks may originate from known malicious user agents or web crawlers. Blocking these can be achieved by utilizing the if directive to match against the "User-Agent" header.

```
1    if ($http_user_agent ~* (badbot|curl|wget)) {
2        return 403;
3    }
```

This configuration blocks requests from user agents that contain the strings 'badbot', 'curl', or 'wget', returning a 403 Forbidden response. The use of the tilde asterisk ~* implies a case-insensitive match.

Implementing Rate Limiting

Rate limiting is a vital feature used to control the amount of allowed requests over a defined time period, significantly reducing the risk of DoS attacks.

```
1    limit_req_zone $binary_remote_addr zone=one:10m rate=1r/s;
```

This line of configuration declares a memory zone named 'one' with a size of 10 megabytes, which tracks requests by IP using the $binary_remote_addr variable. It allows one request per second from each distinct visitor.

Best Practices for Configuring Nginx Firewall

To maximize the effectiveness of Nginx firewall configurations, adhering to the following best practices is recommended:

- Continually update and maintain allow lists and deny lists to ensure that changes in traffic patterns or potential threats are accommodated.

- Apply rate limiting judiciously to prevent unintended denial of service to legitimate users while still protecting against abuse.

- Regularly review access logs to identify and address new sources of malicious traffic.

- Leverage additional modules such as ModSecurity for enhanced firewall capabilities and to provide a web application firewall (WAF) layer.

Configuring Nginx as a firewall is an effective strategy to enhance the security posture of web applications. Through the judicious application of directives and rules, administrators can prevent unauthorized access, mitigate potential attacks, and ensure that web services remain available and reliable.

7.9   Rate Limiting to Prevent Abuse

Rate limiting serves as a crucial defensive mechanism in protecting web applications from various forms of abuse, such as Distributed Denial of Service (DDoS) attacks or brute force login attempts. It effectively controls the rate of requests a user can make to the Nginx server within a specified period. By implementing rate limiting, administrators can thwart attackers attempting to overwhelm the server, thereby safeguarding the application's availability to legitimate users.

Nginx provides built-in directives for configuring rate limiting, leveraging the `limit_req_zone` and `limit_req` directives. The process involves defining a rate limiting zone with `limit_req_zone` in the HTTP block and then applying these limits to specific locations or server blocks using the `limit_req` directive.

```
1  http {
2      limit_req_zone $binary_remote_addr zone=mylimit:10m rate=1r/s;
```

```
3
4    server {
5        location /login {
6            limit_req zone=mylimit burst=5;
7        }
8    }
9  }
```

In this example, a rate limiting zone named mylimit is defined, where $binary_remote_addr is used to track requests by IP address, allocating 10 megabytes of memory for storing these addresses. The rate is set to 1 request per second (1r/s), which means that Nginx permits each IP address to make only one request per second to areas where this limit is applied.

The burst parameter allows for short bursts of requests above the set rate, here permitting up to 5 additional requests to be queued. If the queue exceeds this number, Nginx responds with a 503 Service Unavailable error, effectively throttling excessive requests.

Fine-tuning the burst and rate parameters is essential for balancing protection against abuse while ensuring legitimate users are not unduly restricted. For dynamic applications or APIs where request rates may genuinely vary, adjusting these values based on observed traffic patterns is advisable.

Enforcing rate limits on sensitive endpoints, such as login pages or API endpoints, can significantly mitigate the risk of brute force attacks. Nonetheless, global rate limiting on all paths might inadvertently block legitimate traffic during peak times. Therefore, it's judicious to apply restrictive rate limits selectively, focusing on areas more likely to be targeted by attackers.

```
HTTP/1.1 503 Service Unavailable
Server: nginx
Date: Wed, 10 Mar 2023 12:34:56 GMT
Content-Type: text/html
Content-Length: 169
Connection: close
```

The above demonstrates a typical response from Nginx when rate limits are exceeded. Custom error pages can be configured to improve the user experience in such scenarios, providing information on why the request was blocked and possibly advice on next steps.

Carefully implemented rate limiting can dramatically enhance the security posture of web applications hosted behind an Nginx server. By judiciously setting rate and burst parameters and applying limits to high-risk endpoints, administrators can protect against a plethora of attack vectors while maintaining a positive experience for legitimate users. Regular monitoring and adjustments ensure that these controls remain effective and non-intrusive over time.

7.10   Logging and Monitoring for Security

Logging and monitoring stand as critical components in reinforcing the security of Nginx servers. These practices not only facilitate the detection of potential security incidents but also provide valuable insights for forensic analysis and help in understanding traffic patterns, which can be key in identifying and mitigating threats. This section will discuss configuring Nginx's logging capabilities, adopting monitoring tools, and interpreting log data to enhance security.

To begin with, Nginx offers two types of logs: access logs and error logs. Access logs record every request made to the server, while error logs capture any errors that occur.

- **Access Logs:** These logs are crucial for analyzing the nature of traffic hitting the server.   They can be used to identify suspicious request patterns, such as an unusually high number of requests from a single IP address, which could indicate a brute force attack or a denial of service (DoS) attack attempt.

- **Error Logs:** These logs are invaluable for diagnosing problems within the Nginx server. They can indicate configuration errors, missing files, or more malicious issues like attempts to exploit vulnerabilities in your server or the hosted applications.

Configuring the logging paths in Nginx is straightforward. Below is an example of how to set the paths for both access and error logs in the Nginx configuration file (`nginx.conf`):

```
1  http {
2      access_log /var/log/nginx/access.log;
3      error_log /var/log/nginx/error.log;
4  }
```

Adjusting the verbosity of the error log is possible by adding a logging level next to the error log path. The levels include `debug`, `info`, `notice`, `warn`, `error`, `crit`, `alert`, and `emerg`.

Beyond basic log configuration, analyzing log data is imperative. While manual analysis is possible, it is often impractical for high-traffic sites due to the sheer volume of log entries. Therefore, adopting log analysis tools can be significantly beneficial. Tools such as GoAccess, Logstash, or Elk Stack offer real-time log analysis, enabling the identification of suspicious activities promptly.

```
"192.168.1.1 - - [10/Jul/2023:14:00:00 +0000] "GET /index.html HTTP/1.1" 200 612 "-"
"Mozilla/5.0 (Linux; Android 6.0; Nexus 5 Build/MRA58N) AppleWebKit/537.36
(KHTML, like Gecko) Chrome/86.0.4240.198 Mobile Safari/537.36"
```

The above log entry, extracted from an access log, displays an example of a successful request. Understanding the structure of such entries is crucial in identifying anomalies.

Monitoring tools play a complementary role to logging. Tools like Nagios, Zabbix, or Prometheus can monitor the performance and availability of the Nginx server in real-time. They can alert administrators to issues such as uptime problems, certificate expirations, or resource bottlenecks, often before these issues impact users or security.

Finally, the integration of logging and monitoring into a cohesive security strategy cannot be overstated. Beyond the mere collection of log entries and performance metrics, the real value lies in the continuous analysis of this data, allowing for the timely detection and mitigation of threats. Building a robust logging and monitoring framework is thus essential in maintaining the security and integrity of Nginx servers.

7.11 Understanding and Using Nginx Security Modules

Nginx, as a powerful and versatile web server, extends its functionality through modules that enhance its capability to secure applications and services it hosts. The Nginx Security Modules play a vital part in implementing robust defense mechanisms against various online threats. This section elucidates the primary Nginx modules geared towards security, explaining their configuration and utilization within our Nginx setup.

ModSecurity

ModSecurity, often referred to as an application firewall, provides an array of request filtering and security features, shielding against common web exploits. The module operates by deploying a set of predefined or custom rules that inspect incoming requests and their contents for malicious patterns.

```
1   # Load ModSecurity module
2   load_module modules/ngx_http_modsecurity_module.so;
```

Once loaded, ModSecurity requires the specification of a rule set. The OWASP Core Rule Set (CRS) serves as an excellent starting point, offering comprehensive coverage against widespread web vulnerabilities.

```
1   server {
2       listen 80;
3       server_name mywebsite.com;
4
5       modsecurity on;
6       modsecurity_rules_file /etc/nginx/modsec/main.conf;
7   }
```

Configuration directives within /etc/nginx/modsec/main.conf dictate ModSecurity's behavior, defining which rules to apply and actions to take upon rule violation.

Nginx Naxsi Module

Naxsi (Nginx Anti XSS & SQL Injection) is a high-performance, low-rule-maintenance web application firewall designed to protect against XSS, SQL Injection, and other known threats. Unlike ModSecurity, Naxsi focuses on simplicity and efficiency, employing a positive security model that blocks requests unless explicitly allowed.

```
1  # Add to nginx.conf to load Naxsi module
2  load_module modules/ngx_http_naxsi_module.so;
```

The configuration for Naxsi includes defining a basic set of rules and exceptions tailored to the application it's protecting.

```
1   server {
2       listen 80;
3       server_name myapp.com;
4
5       include /etc/nginx/naxsi_core.rules;
6
7       location / {
8           proxy_pass http://my_backend/;
9           # Check rules for specific location
10          include /etc/nginx/naxsi.rules;
11      }
12  }
```

Rule files, such as `/etc/nginx/naxsi_core.rules`, contain patterns that identify possible attack vectors, instructing Naxsi on how to handle matching requests.

SSL Configuration

Encrypting client-server communications using SSL/TLS is indispensable for web security. Nginx simplifies the implementation of HTTPS, safeguarding data in transit.

```
1   server {
2       listen 443 ssl;
3       server_name mysecuredsite.com;
4
5       ssl_certificate /etc/ssl/mycert.pem;
6       ssl_certificate_key /etc/ssl/mykey.key;
7
8       ssl_protocols TLSv1.2 TLSv1.3;
```

```
 9    ssl_ciphers HIGH:!aNULL:!MD5;
10    }
```

The configuration directives `ssl_certificate` and `ssl_certificate_key` specify the paths to SSL certificate and key files, respectively. The `ssl_protocols` and `ssl_ciphers` directives ensure the use of strong encryption standards and ciphers.

Rate Limiting

Nginx offers built-in support for rate limiting, mitigating DDoS attacks and abusive client behaviors by controlling request rates.

```
1    http {
2        limit_req_zone $binary_remote_addr zone=myzone:10m rate=5r/s;
3
4        server {
5            location /login {
6                limit_req zone=myzone burst=10 nodelay;
7            }
8        }
9    }
```

The `limit_req_zone` directive defines a rate limiting zone, specifying a request rate limit. Requests exceeding this rate or burst limit within a defined location, such as `/login`, are either queued or rejected.

In summary, leveraging Nginx's security modules and features significantly improves the security posture of web applications by introducing multiple layers of defense. Each module addresses specific security concerns, from input validation and encryption to request rate limiting, forming a comprehensive security framework when appropriately configured.

7.12 Regular Updates and Patch Management

Maintaining the security of an Nginx server environment is a continuous process that necessitates diligent attention to the latest software

186

updates and security patches. The rapidly changing landscape of internet security means vulnerabilities can emerge at any time, necessitating a proactive stance on patch management.

Understanding the Importance of Regular Updates

When vulnerabilities in Nginx or its associated libraries are discovered, they are typically addressed promptly by the developers through updates or patches. Ignoring these updates can leave a server exposed to exploits that take advantage of known weaknesses. Thus, integrating regular updates into the server management routine is essential for ensuring ongoing security.

Effective Patch Management Strategies

Effective patch management involves several key practices:

- **Subscription to Security Bulletins:** Staying informed about potential vulnerabilities and the availability of patches is crucial. Administrators should subscribe to Nginx security bulletins and other relevant security news sources to receive timely information.

- **Automated Monitoring for Updates:** Utilizing tools that automatically monitor for updates to Nginx and its dependencies can streamline the patch management process. These tools can notify administrators of critical updates that require immediate attention.

- **Testing Before Deployment:** Before applying updates to a live server, it is wise to test them in a staging environment. This helps identify any potential incompatibilities or issues that could arise, preventing unforeseen disruptions to the service.

- **Scheduled Maintenance Windows:** Establishing regular maintenance windows for applying updates allows for planned downtime (if necessary) and reduces the risk of unanticipated service interruptions.

Automating Security Updates

Automating the process of applying security updates can significantly enhance an organization's security posture. Most operating systems offer tools that can automatically download and install security patches for the system and its software packages, including Nginx. While automation reduces the manual effort involved in keeping the system updated, it's important to balance this with the need for testing updates to prevent issues. A comprehensive approach might include automated alerts for new updates followed by a manual review and testing process before deployment.

Version Control and Rollback Plans

In addition to implementing a robust update policy, maintaining proper version control and planning for rollback in case of faulty updates is crucial. This involves:

- Keeping a log of current and past software versions and configurations.

- Having a backup process in place for quick recovery in the event an update causes problems.

- Documenting update processes and rollback procedures to ensure that they can be executed smoothly if needed.

Nginx Specific Considerations

While general principles of patch management apply, Nginx administrators must also pay attention to:

- The Nginx version in use – ensuring that it is still supported and receiving security updates.

- Configuration changes that may accompany new versions and how they impact existing setups.

- Updates to Nginx modules, which may have their release schedules and security considerations.

A disciplined approach to regular updates and patch management is foundational to securing an Nginx server. By keeping the server and its components up-to-date and by implementing a strategic, automated update process, administrators can significantly mitigate the risk of security vulnerabilities.

Chapter 8

Monitoring and Logging with Nginx

Effective monitoring and logging are pivotal for maintaining the health, performance, and security of web services powered by Nginx. By keeping accurate logs of web server activity and employing real-time monitoring tools, administrators can gain valuable insights into traffic patterns, user behavior, and potential security threats. Nginx provides comprehensive logging capabilities, allowing for detailed access and error logs, which are essential for troubleshooting and optimizing web applications. Additionally, integrating Nginx with external monitoring solutions can facilitate proactive management, ensuring that administrators can swiftly respond to issues as they arise and maintain optimal service levels.

8.1   Introduction to Monitoring and Logging in Nginx

Monitoring and logging in Nginx are critical components for managing the efficiency, security, and reliability of web applications. Nginx, as a high-performance web server, offers extensive capabilities for capturing and analyzing data related to web traffic and server performance. These capabilities provide the foundation for administrators to gain insights and make informed decisions regarding their web services.

Nginx logging can be categorized into two main types: access logs and error logs. Access logs record every request made to the Nginx server, including the requester's IP address, request time, HTTP method, URL, HTTP status code, and more. This comprehensive data captures the behavior of web traffic in detail, facilitating the analysis of user interactions, traffic patterns, and website performance.

```
1   log_format main '$remote_addr - $remote_user [$time_local] "$request" '
2                   '$status $body_bytes_sent "$http_referer" '
3                   '"$http_user_agent" "$http_x_forwarded_for"';
4   access_log /var/log/nginx/access.log main;
```

In the example above, a custom log format named main is defined using various Nginx variables that capture different aspects of the request. This format is then applied to the access log, which is stored at /var/log/nginx/access.log.

Error logs, on the other hand, record information about unexpected events or errors that occur within the server. They are crucial for diagnosing problems in the server configuration or the web applications running on it. By analyzing error logs, administrators can identify and resolve issues more quickly, minimizing the impact on user experience.

```
1   error_log /var/log/nginx/error.log warn;
```

The above line sets the error log path to /var/log/nginx/error.log and configures the logging level to warn, indicating that warning messages and more severe messages will be logged.

Effective monitoring supplements logging by providing real-time insights into the operational state of the Nginx server. Monitoring tools collect data on various performance metrics, such as response times, server load, resource utilization, and more. This information lets administrators identify and respond to potential issues before they impact the service provided to users. Additionally, integrating Nginx with external monitoring solutions can vastly enhance the visibility into the server's health and performance, enabling a more proactive management approach.

To summarize, monitoring and logging in Nginx are indispensable for any administrator aiming to maintain an optimized, secure, and reliable web service. With the appropriate configuration and usage of Nginx's logging capabilities, combined with effective monitoring practices, administrators can safeguard the smooth operation of their web services, ensure quick resolution of issues, and improve overall user satisfaction.

8.2   Understanding Nginx Log Files

Nginx, as a high-performance web server and a reverse proxy, maintains a comprehensive logging mechanism that is instrumental for administrators seeking insights into the operation of their web services. This section will discuss the inherent structure of Nginx log files, focusing on access and error logs, which are fundamental to diagnosing issues and optimizing server performance.

Access Logs

Access logs in Nginx record every request made to the server, detailing crucial information about each transaction. By default, Nginx writes these logs to the file access.log. The information recorded includes the client IP address, the request line from the client, the status code returned by the server, the size of the response sent to the client, and the time taken to serve the request.

Here is an example of a log entry:

```
127.0.0.1 - - [23/Mar/2023:10:55:49 +0000] "GET /index.html HTTP/1.1" 200 612 "-"
"Mozilla/5.0 (X11; Linux x86_64) AppleWebKit/537.36 (KHTML, like Gecko)
Chrome/81.0.4044.122 Safari/537.36"
```

This record signifies a successful request (HTTP status code 200) for /index.html served to a client at IP address 127.0.0.1, using Chrome on Linux. The response size was 612 bytes, and the transaction was completed in a fraction of a second.

Error Logs

Error logs in Nginx document problems encountered while processing requests, including client-requested files not found, server configuration errors, and issues with backend services. Unlike access logs, which primarily track successful interactions, error logs provide visibility into potential problems. By default, Nginx writes the error log to error.log. The log level can be configured to control the verbosity of the log entries, with levels including info, notice, warn, error, crit, alert, and emerg.

As an illustration, consider the following error log entry:

```
2023/03/23 10:59:00 [error] 30039#30039: *1 open() "/usr/share/nginx/html/
not\_found.html" failed (2: No such file or directory), client: 127.0.0.1, server:
localhost, request: "GET /not\_found.html HTTP/1.1", host: "localhost"
```

This entry flags an error where the file not_found.html could not be located (No such file or directory) for a request made by a client from IP address 127.0.0.1. It demonstrates the server's attempt to serve a request, highlighting the issue's nature and the context in which it occurred.

Log Format Configuration

Nginx allows administrators to customize the format of log entries to include information pertinent to their specific needs. Configuration directives in the Nginx configuration file (nginx.conf) enable the specification of custom log formats. For access logs, the directive log_format is used, allowing variables to represent various request and response parameters.

A custom log format might be defined as follows:

```
1  log_format main '$remote_addr - $remote_user [$time_local] "$request" '
2                  '$status $body_bytes_sent "$http_referer" '
3                  '"$http_user_agent" "$http_x_forwarded_for"';
```

This format includes the client IP address ($remote_addr), the time of the request ($time_local), the actual request ($request), the status code ($status), the size of the response ($body_bytes_sent), the referring URL ($http_referer), and the user agent string ($http_user_agent).

Understanding and appropriately configuring Nginx log files not only supports troubleshooting efforts but also aids in performance tuning and threat detection. Through detailed logging, administrators can derive actionable insights to enhance the security, reliability, and efficiency of their web services.

8.3 Configuring Access and Error Logs

Nginx enables the configuration of access and error logs through directives in its configuration files. These logs are crucial as they provide insights into the traffic coming into the server and any issues that the server might encounter.

Location of Configuration Files

Nginx's main configuration file is located at /etc/nginx/nginx.conf. Server-specific configurations can also be found in the /etc/nginx/sites-available/ directory, with symbolic links in the /etc/nginx/sites-enabled/ directory for active configurations.

Access Logs

To configure access logs, the access_log directive is used. This directive can be placed in the http, server, or location contexts. For instance:

```
1  server {
2      server_name mywebsite.com;
3      access_log /var/log/nginx/mywebsite.access.log;
4  }
```

This configuration snippet specifies that requests to mywebsite.com will be logged in the /var/log/nginx/mywebsite.access.log file.

Error Logs

Error logs are configured using the error_log directive. Like the access_log directive, it can be placed in the http, server, or location contexts:

```
1  server {
2      server_name mywebsite.com;
3      error_log /var/log/nginx/mywebsite.error.log;
4  }
```

This configuration will log errors related to mywebsite.com in the /var/log/nginx/mywebsite.error.log file.

Log Format

The default log format for access logs in Nginx is defined by the log_format directive in the http context. To customize, you can specify your format:

```
1  http {
2      log_format main '$remote_addr - $remote_user [$time_local] "$request" '
3                      '$status $body_bytes_sent "$http_referer" '
```

```
4               '"$http_user_agent" "$http_x_forwarded_for"';
5       access_log /var/log/nginx/access.log main;
6   }
```

This custom `main` format includes detailed request information such as the client's IP address, the time of the request, and the user agent.

Log Rotation

Nginx does not handle log rotation natively. Instead, log rotation should be managed by the operating system's log rotation utility, such as `logrotate` on Linux systems. A typical configuration in `/etc/logrotate.d/nginx` might look like this:

```
1   /var/log/nginx/*.log {
2       daily
3       missingok
4       rotate 14
5       compress
6       delaycompress
7       notifempty
8       create 640 nginx adm
9       sharedscripts
10      postrotate
11          [ ! -f /var/run/nginx.pid ] || kill -USR1 `cat /var/run/nginx.pid`
12      endscript
13  }
```

This configuration ensures that logs are rotated daily, kept for two weeks, and that the Nginx master process is signaled to reopen log files after rotation.

Through careful configuration of access and error logs in Nginx, administrators can maintain a detailed record of server activity. This aids in troubleshooting, monitoring, and optimizing server performance.

8.4 Log Rotation and Management

Nginx, like any robust web server, generates a significant amount of log data, primarily through its access and error logs. Over time, these log files can grow considerably, consuming substantial disk space and complicating log analysis. To manage this efficiently, implementing a log rotation system is essential. Log rotation involves periodically closing the current log file, renaming it with a timestamp or sequence number, and then creating a new log file for future entries. This process helps in managing disk space and makes logs more manageable and accessible for analysis.

Implementing Log Rotation in Nginx

Nginx itself does not directly handle log rotation. However, most Unix-like systems, including Linux distributions, come with the `logrotate` utility, which can be configured to manage Nginx log files. To set up `logrotate` for Nginx, a configuration file specific to Nginx logs needs to be created in the `/etc/logrotate.d/` directory.

A basic `logrotate` configuration for Nginx might look like this:

```
/var/log/nginx/*.log {
    daily
    missingok
    rotate 7
    compress
    delaycompress
    notifempty
    create 0640 nginx adm
    sharedscripts
    postrotate
        /usr/sbin/nginx -s reload
    endscript
}
```

The configuration options specify that:

- Logs in /var/log/nginx/ with the extension .log are rotated daily.

- Up to 7 old log files are kept.

- Compressed to save space, except for the latest log file.

- Permissions are set to ensure that files are readable only by the Nginx user and group for security reasons.

- The Nginx service is gracefully reloaded after log rotation to ensure logging continues without interruption.

Understanding Log Rotation Options

The configuration options provided in the `logrotate` utility offer flexibility in managing log files:

- `daily`, `weekly`, `monthly` control the frequency of log rotation.

- `rotate` defines the number of old log files to keep.

- `compress` and `delaycompress` help manage disk space by compressing old log files.

- `missingok` avoids errors if no log files are found.

- `notifempty` prevents the rotation of empty log files.

- `create` defines the permissions and ownership of the new log file.

Careful configuration of these options is crucial for ensuring that log files are rotated and managed in a manner that suits the specific needs of the environment and maintains the availability and integrity of logging data.

Log Rotation Best Practices

To ensure optimal performance and reliability of log management, a few best practices should be followed:

- Regularly verify the `logrotate` configuration to ensure it meets evolving logging requirements and disk space constraints.

- Monitor disk space usage closely, especially on systems with high traffic volumes, as logs can grow rapidly.

- Consider integrating log management within a broader system monitoring and alerting framework to proactively address issues related to log file size and rotation.

- In high-availability environments, ensure that log rotation actions, such as reloading or restarting Nginx, do not adversely affect service availability.

Managing log files through rotation is a critical aspect of Nginx administration. Effectively configuring and automating log rotation ensures that logs are retained for an appropriate amount of time while minimizing disk space usage and preserving the performance and stability of the web server.

8.5   Analyzing Log Files with Third-Party Tools

Nginx log files, comprising access and error logs, contain a wealth of information that can be leveraged to enhance web application performance, security, and user experience. However, raw log files are often voluminous and challenging to interpret manually. Thus, the utilization of third-party tools for log analysis emerges as an invaluable practice for extracting actionable insights efficiently.

Choosing the Right Tool

Selecting an appropriate log analysis tool hinges on several factors, including the specific requirements of the web service, the complexity of the web application, and the desired granularity of the insights. Commonly used third-party tools include GoAccess, ELK Stack (Elasticsearch, Logstash, Kibana), and Graylog. Each tool offers unique features and caters to different analysis needs.

- **GoAccess** provides real-time log analysis in a terminal-based interface, making it suitable for quick insights and environments where GUI is not preferred or available.

- **ELK Stack** combines powerful data ingestion (Logstash), storage and indexing (Elasticsearch), and visualization (Kibana) capabilities, allowing for deep, customizable analysis of large datasets.

- **Graylog** offers a user-friendly web interface for log management and analysis, supporting powerful search queries and dashboards for visualizing data.

Integration Process

To analyze Nginx logs with these third-party tools, an integration process is typically required. This process involves directing Nginx log output to the chosen tool and configuring the tool to correctly parse and display the log data. The integration steps vary depending on the tool but generally follow a similar pattern.

1. Configure Nginx to ensure that log files are in a format compatible with the analysis tool. This might involve customizing the log format in `nginx.conf`.

2. Set up the log analysis tool according to its documentation. For tools like ELK Stack, this involves setting up Logstash to ingest logs, Elasticsearch to store and index data, and Kibana for visualization.

3. Direct Nginx log output to the analysis tool. This can be achieved through file-based log shipping, syslog forwarding, or using dedicated log shippers such as Filebeat for ELK Stack.

Extracting Insights

Once integration is complete, the analysis tool can begin processing Nginx log data. Here are some examples of insights that can be extracted:

201

- **User Behavior:** Analyzing access logs to identify the most frequently accessed URLs, peak traffic times, and geographical distribution of visitors.

- **Performance Issues:** Using error logs to pinpoint recurring server errors, slow-loading resources, and potential bottlenecks in web application performance.

- **Security Threats:** Identifying patterns indicative of security threats, such as repeated access attempts from a single IP address or suspiciously high volumes of traffic to sensitive endpoints.

To visually represent these insights, tools like Kibana and Graylog can be used to create dashboards that update in real-time, presenting a clear overview of web server health, performance, and security posture.

Leveraging third-party tools for Nginx log analysis dramatically simplifies the process of monitoring and optimizing web services. By automating data ingestion, parsing, and visualization, these tools enable administrators to swiftly identify and respond to issues, ensuring that Nginx-based applications continue to deliver optimal performance and security.

8.6   Real-Time Monitoring Options

Monitoring Nginx in real-time involves employing tools that provide immediate feedback on the web server's performance and status. This immediate feedback enables administrators to quickly identify and address issues, ensuring the smooth operation of the web service. Real-time monitoring tools can offer insights into request rates, response times, active connections, and system resource utilization among other metrics.

One of the essential tools for real-time monitoring of Nginx is `NGINX Amplify`. `NGINX Amplify` is a SaaS-based monitoring tool that provides comprehensive analytics about Nginx performance, including detailed metrics on web server activity, error identification, and performance optimization.

```
1   # Installation steps for NGINX Amplify Agent
2   curl -L https://github.com/nginxinc/nginx-amplify-agent/raw/master/packages/
        install.sh | bash
```

After installation, the NGINX Amplify Agent starts collecting data and transmitting it to the NGINX Amplify dashboard, where the data is visualized through graphs and tables. Users can configure alerts based on specific metrics exceeding thresholds, enabling proactive issue resolution.

Another critical tool for real-time metrics is the Stub Status module. This open-source module provides basic metrics about Nginx, including the number of active connections and details about the requests being processed. To enable the Stub Status module, the following block needs to be added to the Nginx configuration file.

```
1   server {
2       listen 8080;
3       location /nginx_status {
4           stub_status on;
5           # Security: Only allow access from the localhost
6           allow 127.0.0.1;
7           deny all;
8       }
9   }
```

When configuration adjustments complete, metrics become accessible by accessing the /nginx_status endpoint, providing a snapshot of the current performance.

```
Active connections: 291
server accepts handled requests
 7368 7368 10993
Reading: 6 Writing: 179 Waiting: 106
```

The output details the number of active connections and provides a breakdown of the number of requests being processed.

Another popular real-time monitoring solution is Telegraf with InfluxDB and Grafana. This combination allows for the collection, storage, and visualization of Nginx performance data.

- Telegraf collects system and Nginx metrics.

- InfluxDB serves as the time-series database to store the collected metrics.

- Grafana provides a powerful dashboard for visualizing the metrics and setting up alerts.

To integrate Nginx with Telegraf, the following input plugin configuration is used in the Telegraf configuration file:

```
[[inputs.nginx]]
  urls = ["http://localhost/nginx_status"]
```

Real-time monitoring of Nginx offers the advantage of immediate insight into the web server's operation, enabling swift responses to any arising issues. By implementing and utilizing such monitoring tools, administrators can significantly improve the reliability and performance of their Nginx-powered web services.

8.7   Integrating Nginx with External Monitoring Tools

Integrating Nginx with external monitoring tools greatly enhances the ability to track the performance and health of Nginx servers in real-time. This section delves into various strategies and tools available for such integration, focusing on the advantages of using external monitoring systems over relying solely on internal logs and metrics.

Nginx, by its design, offers extensive logging capabilities that provide insights into server performance and potential issues. However, deciphering these logs and making real-time decisions can be challenging. External monitoring tools specialize in collecting, aggregating, and analyzing data from various sources, including Nginx, to offer a holistic view of the system's health and performance.

Advantages of Using External Monitoring Tools

- **Real-time alerts and notifications:** External tools can monitor Nginx logs and metrics in real-time, providing immediate alerts about potential issues, such as high traffic loads or error rates.

- **Comprehensive data visualization:** These tools typically offer dashboards that visualize complex data, making it easier to understand traffic patterns, user behavior, and performance trends.

- **Automated log analysis:** Automating the analysis of access and error logs helps in quickly identifying the causes of slowdowns or failures.

- **Integration with other systems:** Monitoring tools can aggregate data from various parts of the infrastructure, not limited to Nginx, offering a comprehensive overview of the entire system's health.

Popular External Monitoring Tools

Several external monitoring tools are well-suited for integration with Nginx. Some noteworthy options are:

- **Prometheus** is an open-source system monitoring and alerting toolkit widely used in the industry. Its robust querying language and efficient time series database make it an excellent choice for monitoring Nginx performance metrics.

- **Grafana** provides powerful and customizable dashboards for data visualization. Although it does not collect data by itself, Grafana can be integrated with data sources like Prometheus to display Nginx metrics in an informative and visually appealing manner.

- **Datadog** offers a cloud-based monitoring and analytics platform. It supports automatic detection of Nginx instances and provides extensive metrics, logs, and real-time interactive dashboards.

- **Elastic Stack** (formerly known as ELK Stack) combines Elastic-search, Logstash, and Kibana to offer logging, log analysis, and visualization capabilities. It is particularly useful for analyzing Nginx access and error logs.

Steps for Integrating Nginx with Prometheus and Grafana

The integration of Nginx with Prometheus for monitoring and Grafana for visualization involves several steps. Here is a brief overview:

1. Ensure that the Nginx `stub_status` module is enabled. This module provides access to basic status information about Nginx.

2. Configure Prometheus to scrape metrics from Nginx. This requires editing the Prometheus configuration file to add Nginx as a target.

3. Install and configure the `nginx_exporter`. This tool translates metrics from Nginx's native format into a format Prometheus can understand.

4. Set up a Grafana instance and configure it to use Prometheus as a data source.

5. Import or create a dashboard in Grafana tailored to visualize Nginx metrics, offering insights into request rates, response times, and error rates.

This integration enables administrators to monitor Nginx servers with high granularity, facilitating proactive management of web services. The process might vary slightly depending on the specific environment and versions of the software used.

By integrating Nginx with external monitoring tools, administrators can significantly improve the observability of web services. This practice not only aids in maintaining optimal performance but also supports troubleshooting efforts and enhances the security posture of the infrastructure.

8.8 Performance Metrics to Monitor in Nginx

In web server management, understanding and monitoring key performance metrics is crucial for ensuring that Nginx operates at peak efficiency. These metrics provide insights into the health, responsiveness, and reliability of Nginx, enabling administrators to make informed decisions about optimizations and configurations. This section will elucidate several pivotal metrics that should be under constant surveillance.

- **Requests Per Second (RPS)**: This metric indicates the number of HTTP requests that Nginx handles within a second. High values for RPS signify heavy client traffic and are an indicator of how well the web server is performing under load.

- **Connection Statistics**: Nginx manages two types of connections: active and waiting. Active connections include all current connections, whereas waiting connections are those that have been processed and await a response. Monitoring these statistics provides insight into the volume of traffic being managed and the efficiency of connection handling.

  - `Active Connections`: Total number of active client connections.
  - `Waiting Connections`: Current connections that have finished processing and are awaiting further actions.

- **Error Rate**: This is quantified by the number of error responses (4xx and 5xx HTTP status codes) served by Nginx. An increasing trend in error rates may indicate configuration issues, resource limitations, or upstream server problems.

- **Memory Usage**: The amount of memory (RAM) that Nginx is utilizing is critical, especially in a constrained environment. Efficient memory usage ensures that Nginx can handle more connections and serve more content without necessitating additional computing resources.

- **CPU Load**: Similar to memory usage, the CPU load metrics signify how much processor time Nginx consumes. Monitoring CPU load is crucial for preventing server overload and ensuring that there is sufficient processing power available for handling incoming requests.

- **Throughput**: This refers to the volume of data transferred over a specific period. Throughput is measured in bytes and provides insights into the amount of content being served by Nginx. It is a useful metric for bandwidth management and planning.

For real-time monitoring of these metrics, utilizing tools such as ngx_http_status_module or integrating Nginx with external monitoring solutions like Prometheus can provide comprehensive insights. These tools facilitate the collection, analysis, and visualization of performance metrics, thus empowering administrators with the data required to optimize Nginx configurations, scale resources as needed, and identify potential bottlenecks before they affect the user experience.

To exemplify obtaining basic statistics from Nginx, one can utilize the ngx_http_status_module. The configuration snippet below illustrates how to enable the ngx_http_status_module in the Nginx configuration:

```
1  location /nginx_status {
2      stub_status on;
3      access_log off;
4      allow 127.0.0.1; # allow access from localhost
5      deny all; # deny access from all other IPs
6  }
```

Accessing this endpoint from the command line with a tool like curl, by executing curl http://127.0.0.1/nginx_status, yields output similar to the following:

208

```
Active connections: 43
server accepts handled requests
 7368 7368 10993
Reading: 0 Writing: 5 Waiting: 38
```

This output provides immediate insights into the current state of the web server, showcasing the total number of active connections, and the read, write, and wait states of these connections. Monitoring trends in these figures over time is essential for assessing the impact of configuration changes and the health of Nginx under various load conditions.

8.9 Troubleshooting Common Issues with Logs

Troubleshooting issues within Nginx logs necessitates a structured approach, as logs are often the first indication of a problem within web services. Although Nginx logging capabilities are robust, administrators may encounter several common issues that can complicate troubleshooting efforts. Understanding these issues is paramount in diagnosing and resolving problems efficiently.

Identifying Errors in Access and Error Logs

The foundation of effective log analysis in Nginx lies in distinguishing between access logs and error logs. Access logs record all requests processed by the Nginx server, whereas error logs capture issues encountered during the handling of these requests. Errors present in logs can vary widely, from client-side errors indicated by 4xx status codes to server-side issues reflected by 5xx status codes.

```
1   # Example of a client-side error in an access log
2   127.0.0.1 - - [12/Mar/2023:14:22:38 +0000] "GET /nonexistent-page.html HTTP/1.1"
        404 152 "-" "Mozilla/5.0"
3
4   # Example of a server-side error in an error log
5   2023/03/12 14:22:38 [error] 318#318: *42 open() "/usr/share/nginx/html/
        nonexistent-page.html" failed (2: No such file or directory), client:
```

```
127.0.0.1, server: localhost, request: "GET /nonexistent-page.html HTTP
/1.1", host: "localhost"
```

Decoding Log Message Content

Effective troubleshooting involves not just identifying errors but comprehending their context. Error logs in Nginx provide detailed information, including the timestamp of the error, the severity level, process ID, and a descriptive message about the error. Understanding these components can significantly aid in pinpointing the source of a problem.

Log File Size and Management Issues

One common issue with Nginx logs is their potential to grow significantly in size, especially on high-traffic websites. Large log files can become unwieldy, consuming substantial disk space and making log analysis increasingly difficult. Implementing log rotation, a process that automatically archives old logs and creates new ones at specified intervals, is a critical strategy for managing log sizes effectively. Nginx supports log rotation natively or through external utilities such as `logrotate`.

Missing Log Entries

In some cases, administrators may notice missing log entries, which can occur for several reasons, including incorrect log configuration or file permissions issues. Ensuring that the `access_log` and `error_log` directives are correctly specified in the Nginx configuration files is crucial. Additionally, verifying that Nginx has the necessary permissions to write to the specified log files is essential for preventing data loss.

Analyzing High Volume of Error Codes

A sudden surge in specific error codes, such as 502 (Bad Gateway) or 504 (Gateway Timeout), can indicate underlying issues with backend services or network connectivity. In such instances, correlating the timing of these errors with changes in infrastructure or application deployments can provide valuable insights into the root cause.

Security-Related Log Entries

Security-related entries in Nginx logs, such as repeated access attempts to sensitive areas of a web application, should be monitored closely. Identifying patterns in these entries, such as the source IP address or requested URLs, can help in detecting and mitigating potential security threats.

```
172.16.0.1 - - [12/Mar/2023:14:22:38 +0000] "POST /admin/login.php HTTP/1.1" 200
1745 "-" "Mozilla/5.0"
```

Resolving Issues with Log Interpretation

When encountering difficulties in interpreting log files, third-party log analysis tools can provide a more intuitive interface for sifting through large volumes of log data. Tools such as GoAccess, Logstash, and Kibana offer powerful features for filtering, searching, and visualizing log data, significantly simplifying the troubleshooting process.

By systematically addressing these common issues with Nginx logs, administrators can enhance their ability to diagnose and resolve problems, ensuring the smooth operation of web services.

8.10   Security Considerations in Logging

Security is a crucial aspect of web server maintenance, making it vital to understand the security considerations associated with logging in

Nginx. By effectively managing log files, administrators can protect sensitive data, ensure compliance with legal and regulatory obligations, and detect potential security threats early on.

Sensitive Information in Logs

Nginx logs can inadvertently contain sensitive information, such as usernames, passwords, or personal data, which could be exploited if accessed by malicious actors. To mitigate this risk, it's important to:

- Regularly audit log files for unintentional logging of sensitive information.

- Utilize Nginx's log formatting options to exclude or obscure sensitive data. For example, using set $sanitized_param ***; can help to replace sensitive parameters with asterisks or another placeholder.

Access Control and File Permissions

Restricting access to Nginx log files is essential to safeguard the information they contain. Set strict file permissions to prevent unauthorized access:

```
chmod 640 /var/log/nginx/access.log
chmod 640 /var/log/nginx/error.log
```

These commands modify the log files' permissions so that only the owner and members of the group can read and write, while others have no permissions.

Log Encryption

For enhanced security, especially in compliance-driven environments or when logs contain particularly sensitive information, consider encrypting your log files. Encryption can be implemented at the filesystem level or by piping logs through an encryption tool before writing them to disk.

```
1   cat /var/log/nginx/access.log | gzip | openssl enc -aes-256-cbc -e > access.
        log.enc
```

This example illustrates a simple pipeline for compressing and encrypting the access.log file using AES-256 encryption.

Integration with Security Information and Event Management (SIEM)

To further enhance the security posture, integrating Nginx logs with a Security Information and Event Management (SIEM) system can provide comprehensive visibility into potential security incidents across the network. SIEM systems allow for:

- Real-time analysis and correlation of log data from different sources.

- Automated alerting based on predefined criteria, aiding in the quick detection of security breaches or anomalies.

- Advanced data protection compliance capabilities, crucial for industries regulated by GDPR, HIPAA, or other privacy standards.

Regular Log Auditing

Regular auditing of Nginx logs aids in early detection of suspicious activities and potential security threats. Effective log auditing involves:

- Establishing a routine schedule for reviewing logs.

- Using automated tools to scan for common patterns indicative of security concerns, such as multiple failed login attempts or requests for resources that do not exist.

- Documenting findings and taking appropriate action to address any vulnerabilities or breaches.

To conclude, maintaining a strong security posture in relation to Nginx logging demands constant vigilance, regular auditing, and adherence to best practices in log management. By taking steps to secure log files, filter sensitive information, and integrate with broader security systems, administrators can significantly enhance the security and reliability of their web services.

8.11   Alerting Based on Log Analysis

Alerting based on log analysis is a critical process that transitions passive observation into active response mechanisms within Nginx environments. The objective here is to automate the detection of specific patterns, anomalies, or thresholds within log files that could indicate performance issues, security threats, or system failures. By implementing alerting mechanisms, administrators can receive instantaneous notifications about significant events, enabling quick reaction times that can mitigate potential damage or restore services more rapidly.

To establish an effective alerting system, the following steps are crucial:

- **Define meaningful alert conditions:** Identifying which log entries or patterns are significant for your environment is the first step. This could range from detecting HTTP error codes such as 500 (Internal Server Error) or 404 (Not Found) in access logs, to identifying certain text strings within error logs that indicate specific failure modes.

- **Set appropriate thresholds:**   For conditions that are quantifiable, determining thresholds that trigger alerts is necessary.   For instance, alerting might be configured for when the number of 500 status codes surpasses a certain count within a given timeframe, suggesting a severe problem with the web application.

- **Choose your alerting mechanisms:** There are numerous ways to receive alerts, including emails, SMS messages, or even integration with incident management systems via APIs. The choice depends on the gravity of alerts and the communication preferences within your team.

- **Configure log parsing and analysis tools:** Since raw log files can be difficult to monitor in real-time, leveraging tools that can parse, filter, and analyze log data is crucial. Common tools for this task include ELK Stack (Elasticsearch, Logstash, Kibana) or Splunk, where log data can be ingested, analyzed, and matched against defined alert conditions.

- **Test and refine:** After setting up alert conditions and mechanisms, thorough testing is required to ensure accuracy and to minimize false positives or negatives. Regular refinement based on real-world feedback will help tune the sensitivity and specificity of alerts.

Implementing an Alert in Logstash Configuration Example:

For illustration, consider setting up a simple alert for detecting an excessive number of 500 status codes in Nginx access logs using Logstash.

```
1  filter {
2    if [response] == "500" {
3      grok {
4        match => { "message" => "%{IPORHOST:clientip} %{USER:ident} %{USER:auth}
              \[%{HTTPDATE:timestamp}\] \"%{WORD:method} %{URIPATHPARAM:request}
              HTTP/%{NUMBER:httpversion}\" %{NUMBER:response} (?:%{NUMBER:bytes}|-)"
            }
5      }
6      throttle {
7        period => 60
8        after_count => 100
9        key => "%{clientip}"
10       add_tag => "throttled"
11     }
12   }
13 }
14
15 output {
```

```
16   if "throttled" in [tags] {
17     email {
18       to => "admin@example.com"
19       subject => "Alert: High number of 500 errors detected"
20       body => "Threshold exceeded: More than 100 HTTP 500 responses in the last
               minute."
21       via => "sendmail"
22     }
23   }
24 }
```

In this configuration, Logstash filters access logs for HTTP 500 response codes. Using the `throttle` filter, it triggers an email alert if more than 100 occurrences are detected within a 60-second period, indicative of a potential issue that requires immediate attention.

Setting up alerting based on log analysis in Nginx is a proactive measure to maintain the reliability, performance, and security of web services. By defining meaningful alert conditions, setting appropriate thresholds, choosing effective alerting mechanisms, configuring log parsing and analysis tools, and continuously testing and refining these parameters, administrators can significantly enhance their capability to preempt and respond to critical incidents in a timely manner. Integrating such alerts fosters a more resilient web ecosystem, where potential issues are identified and mitigated before they escalate into more serious problems.

8.12   Customizing Log Formats for Advanced Analysis

Customizing log formats in Nginx is a key step for conducting advanced analysis, empowering administrators with the ability to tailor logs to meet specific monitoring requirements. This customization enables the extraction of valuable insights from the web server's operations, providing data that can aid in performance tuning, security assessments, and understanding user behavior.

To begin customizing log formats, one must first understand the configuration directive involved: `log_format`. This directive is placed inside the `http` block of the Nginx configuration file. A customized log format is defined by specifying a name for the format followed by the variables and strings that should be logged. Here's a basic syntax example:

```
http {
    log_format main '$remote_addr - $remote_user [$time_local] "$request" '
                    '$status $body_bytes_sent "$http_referer" '
                    '"$http_user_agent" "$http_x_forwarded_for"';
}
```

In this example, a log format named main is defined. The variables such as $remote_addr and $remote_user are placeholders that Nginx will replace with actual data when logging requests. This includes client IP addresses, user identifiers, timestamps, request details, response statuses, and more.

After defining a custom log format, it must be applied to an access log. The access_log directive is used for this purpose, which can be placed within the http, server, or location blocks. By doing so, it specifies where the logs should be written and which format to use. Here is how to apply the previously defined main format:

```
access_log /path/to/your/log/file.log main;
```

It's worth mentioning the versatility of the log_format directive, which supports including arbitrary text in logs. For instance, administrators might want to add fixed-string markers or notes to logs for easier parsing or flag specific types of requests.

Additionally, creating more complex log formats can involve conditional logging using the if directive or embedding variables that calculate values at the time of logging. This is particularly useful for tracking metrics such as request processing times, as shown below:

```
log_format timing '[$time_local] "$request" $status '
               'Request time: $request_time ms';
```

This custom format logs each request's timestamp, request line, status code, and the time taken to process the request in milliseconds.

Utilizing custom log formats in Nginx allows for a much richer data collection, which is indispensable for detailed analysis. Whether through manual log analysis, scripting, or integration with third-party log analysis tools, the insights gained can dramatically improve an application's performance, enhance security, and offer a better understanding of the user experience.

To demonstrate the potential of customized logging, consider a scenario where an administrator needs to investigate intermittent performance issues. By analyzing logs with custom formats that include request processing times and specific error codes, the administrator can identify patterns that might indicate the root cause, such as requests that consistently take longer to process or endpoints that frequently return errors.

Customizing log formats according to specific analytical needs unlocks the full potential of Nginx's logging capabilities. It lays a foundation for effective monitoring, troubleshooting, and optimizing web applications, ensuring that they meet the performance and reliability standards expected by users and stakeholders alike.

Chapter 9

Performance Tuning and Optimization

Performance tuning and optimization in Nginx focus on adjusting server configurations to improve the efficiency, speed, and scalability of web applications. This involves optimizing connection handling, managing resources effectively, and implementing caching and content compression mechanisms. By fine-tuning various Nginx settings—such as worker processes, buffer sizes, and timeout values—administrators can significantly enhance the performance of their web services. These optimizations ensure that Nginx can handle high traffic volumes with minimal latency, providing a seamless experience for end-users while minimizing resource consumption on the server side.

9.1 Basics of Web Performance

Understanding the fundamentals of web performance is crucial for effectively configuring Nginx to serve web applications efficiently. Performance, in the context of web applications, refers to how quickly and responsively web pages are delivered to the user's browser. Key factors that influence web performance include latency, bandwidth, and the server's ability to handle concurrent connections efficiently.

Latency and Bandwidth

Latency is the delay from the initiation of a request to the moment the response begins to arrive. This delay is a critical component of web performance and is influenced by physical distance between the client and server, the speed of the server's response, and routing infrastructure.

Bandwidth, on the other hand, is the maximum rate of data transfer across a given path. While higher bandwidth can improve the speed of data delivery, its impact on web performance is most notable when large files are being transferred. In many real-world scenarios, especially on modern high-speed internet connections, latency rather than bandwidth becomes the limiting factor in perceived web performance.

```
# Example of a basic Nginx directive to set up gzip compression,
# which can improve latency by reducing file sizes
gzip on;
gzip_types text/plain application/xml application/json;
```

Connection Handling

Efficient connection handling is paramount for optimizing web performance. Nginx shines in this area due to its event-driven architecture, allowing it to handle thousands of concurrent connections with minimal resource consumption. The worker_processes and worker_connections directives in Nginx's configuration play a vital role in determining how effectively it can manage connections.

```
worker_processes auto; # Utilize all CPU cores
worker_connections 1024; # Number of connections per worker
```

Each worker_process can handle up to the number of connections specified by worker_connections, with the total capacity being the product of these two values. Optimizing these settings based on the server's hardware and expected traffic can significantly improve performance.

The Role of Caching

Caching is another crucial aspect of web performance. By storing copies of frequently accessed resources, such as HTML pages, images, and CSS files, Nginx can reduce the need to generate or fetch these resources from the backend on each request. This both lowers server load and decreases response times.

```
1   # Example of configuring caching in Nginx
2   location ~* \.(jpg|jpeg|png|gif|ico|css|js)\$ {
3       expires 30d;
4       add_header Cache-Control "public, immutable";
5   }
```

The expires directive specifies how long the resource should be cached by the client or proxy, while Cache-Control further fine-tunes caching behavior. Implementing effective caching strategies is essential for high-performance web applications.

Performance Metrics

When measuring web performance, several metrics are of particular interest:

- **Time to First Byte (TTFB)**: The time from the client sending a request to receiving the first byte of the response. This metric is crucial for understanding server response times.

- **Fully Loaded Time**: The total time it takes for a page and all its resources to fully load. This metric reflects the end-to-end user experience.

- **Concurrent Connections**: The number of connections a server

221

can handle simultaneously before performance degrades. This metric helps in sizing server capacity.

Optimization of web performance is multi-faceted, requiring careful consideration of server configuration, network characteristics, and application design. Nginx provides a flexible and powerful platform for addressing these challenges, but understanding the underlying principles of web performance is essential for effective optimization.

9.2 Optimizing Nginx Configuration for Speed

Optimizing the configuration of Nginx for speed is an essential step in ensuring that your web services are delivered efficiently. This process involves adjusting several key parameters within the Nginx configuration file, which can have a significant impact on performance. In this section, we will dissect these optimization techniques, focusing on worker processes, buffer sizes, timeout settings, and the use of the keepalive directive.

Worker Processes and Worker Connections

The worker_processes directive dictates the number of worker processes that Nginx will spawn. The optimal setting for this directive usually matches the number of CPU cores available on the system. This alignment allows Nginx to fully utilize the hardware, enhancing parallel processing capabilities.

```
1  worker_processes auto;
```

Additionally, the worker_connections directive configures the maximum number of simultaneous connections that each worker process can handle. A recommended approach is to set this value to a high number to accommodate as many connections as possible, keeping in mind the limits imposed by the operating system.

```
1  worker_connections 1024;
```

Adjusting Buffer Sizes

Nginx uses buffers for storing data from client requests and responses to and from the server. Optimizing these buffer sizes can significantly reduce memory consumption and improve response times. The key directives to adjust include client_body_buffer_size, client_header_buffer_size, and large_client_header_buffers.

```
1  client_body_buffer_size 16k;
2  client_header_buffer_size 1k;
3  large_client_header_buffers 4 8k;
```

These settings help Nginx to efficiently handle client requests by allocating appropriate memory resources, thereby speeding up request processing.

Configuring Timeouts

Proper management of timeout settings can prevent resource wastage on connections that are no longer active. The keepalive_timeout directive specifies how long an idle keepalive connection remains open. A lower value helps in freeing up server resources more quickly.

```
1  keepalive_timeout 65;
```

Moreover, the send_timeout and client_body_timeout directives determine the maximum time Nginx waits for data transmission and for the client's request body to be received, respectively.

```
1  send_timeout 2;
2  client_body_timeout 12;
```

Utilizing Keepalive Connections

Enabling keepalive connections in Nginx can enhance the speed of subsequent requests between the same client and server by reusing the established connection. The `keepalive_requests` directive allows you to specify the maximum number of requests that can be sent over a single keepalive connection.

```
1  keepalive_requests 100;
```

This reuse of connections reduces the overhead of establishing new connections for each request, thus improving the overall speed of web service delivery.

By meticulously adjusting these directives in the Nginx configuration file, administrators can achieve optimal performance, ensuring that web applications are served swiftly, efficiently, and with minimal resource consumption. These optimizations are crucial for achieving high performance and scalability in any web-serving environment facilitated by Nginx.

9.3 Tuning TCP/IP Settings for Performance

Tuning TCP/IP settings is a critical aspect of optimizing Nginx server performance. TCP/IP, the backbone protocol of the Internet, controls how data is transmitted across networks. By adjusting TCP/IP parameters, administrators can significantly improve Nginx's handling of client connections and data flow. This section will discuss key TCP/IP settings that can be optimized for performance.

Adjusting TCP Buffer Sizes

One of the primary adjustments in tuning TCP/IP for Nginx involves modifying the TCP buffer sizes. The buffer sizes determine how much data can be in transit during network communication. Appropriately sized buffers can enhance throughput and reduce latency.

```
1   # Set TCP Buffer Sizes
2   net.core.rmem_max = 16777216
3   net.core.wmem_max = 16777216
4   net.ipv4.tcp_rmem = 4096 87380 16777216
5   net.ipv4.tcp_wmem = 4096 65536 16777216
```

These settings adjust the maximum read and write memory allocations for TCP sockets, improving the efficiency of data transmission.

Enabling TCP Fast Open

TCP Fast Open (TFO) allows the sending of data during the initial SYN handshake of the TCP connection, reducing the overall latency of the connection setup. To enable TFO, the following configuration can be applied:

```
1   # Enable TCP Fast Open
2   net.ipv4.tcp_fastopen = 3
```

Setting the value to 3 enables TFO for both incoming and outgoing connections, providing a boost in performance for Nginx, especially for TLS/SSL content delivery where connection setup times are crucial.

Optimizing TCP Keepalive Intervals

TCP Keepalive is a mechanism to check whether a connection is still valid, helping avoid unnecessary retransmissions for lost or dead connections. Adjusting the keepalive interval can optimize resource usage and improve connection stability.

```
1   # Set TCP Keepalive Time
2   net.ipv4.tcp_keepalive_time = 600
3   net.ipv4.tcp_keepalive_probes = 5
4   net.ipv4.tcp_keepalive_intvl = 60
```

These settings reduce the keepalive time to 10 minutes, with probes sent every 60 seconds after an initial failure, ensuring that idle connections are detected and recycled more efficiently.

Increasing the Backlog Queue

The backlog queue size determines how many incoming connections can be pending before Nginx starts rejecting new requests. Increasing this limit can help Nginx handle sudden spikes in web traffic.

```
1  # Increase Backlog Queue
2  net.core.somaxconn = 4096
```

Setting the backlog queue size to a higher value allows Nginx to queue more connection requests, minimizing the chances of connection timeouts during peak loads.

By fine-tuning these TCP/IP settings, Nginx administrators can significantly enhance the server's ability to manage high volumes of traffic with improved connection stability and reduced latency. It's important to note that the optimal values for these settings may vary depending on the specific hardware, network environment, and workload characteristics. Therefore, administrators should perform thorough testing before applying these changes to production environments.

9.4   Content Compression and Gzip Settings

Content compression is a critical aspect of web performance optimization. It allows the server to provide smaller file sizes which are faster to transmit over the network. This leads to reduced bandwidth usage and improved load times for end-users. Nginx supports various types of compression, but one of the most effective and widely used methods is Gzip. In this section, we will discuss how to configure Gzip in Nginx to enhance web application performance.

Gzip compression works by finding similar strings within a text file and replacing them temporarily, making the data smaller. The browser of the end-user then decompresses the data upon receipt, rendering the original content. This technique is particularly effective for compressing HTML, CSS, and JavaScript files, which often contain abundant repetitive text data.

To enable Gzip compression in Nginx, specific directives must be added or adjusted in the Nginx configuration file. Typically, these configurations are placed in the http{} block to apply them globally across all server blocks (virtual servers). However, they can also be specified within an individual server{} or location{} block to limit their scope.

The key directives for configuring Gzip compression are as follows:

- gzip: Enables or disables Gzip compression. Set this to on to activate compression.

- gzip_types: Specifies MIME types that should be compressed. Common types include text/plain, text/css, application/json, application/javascript, and others.

- gzip_min_length: Sets the minimum response length to engage compression. Responses smaller than this threshold will not be compressed.

- gzip_comp_level: Determines the compression level, ranging from 1 (least compression, fastest) to 9 (most compression, slowest). A higher compression level means smaller files but requires more processing power.

- gzip_buffers: Sets the number and size of buffers used to compress responses. Adjusting this can optimize the memory footprint during compression.

- gzip_http_version: Specifies the minimum HTTP version of a request to compress. Typically set to 1.1.

- gzip_proactive: Enables proactive compression even for connections that do not explicitly request it via the Accept-Encoding header.

Here is an example configuration that activates Gzip compression for commonly compressed types, with a moderate compression level and default settings for other parameters:

```
1  http {
2      gzip on;
3      gzip_types text/plain text/css application/json application/javascript;
4      gzip_min_length 256;
5      gzip_comp_level 4;
6      gzip_buffers 16 8k;
7      gzip_http_version 1.1;
8  }
```

Effective use of Gzip compression requires a balance between compression ratio and CPU usage. A higher `gzip_comp_level` can reduce the file size further, but the incremental benefits diminish, and CPU cost increases. It's recommended to experiment with different levels to find an optimal configuration for your specific environment.

After configuring Gzip, it is crucial to verify that compression is working correctly. This can be done by inspecting the `Content-Encoding` header in the response using browser developer tools or command-line tools like `curl`. A response from the server with `Content-Encoding: gzip` indicates that Gzip compression is effectively applied.

```
$ curl -I -H "Accept-Encoding: gzip" http://example.com
HTTP/1.1 200 OK
Content-Encoding: gzip
...
```

Implementing Gzip compression is a straightforward yet powerful way to enhance the speed and responsiveness of your Nginx-hosted web applications. By carefully tuning the Gzip settings as outlined above, you can significantly improve the user experience for your site visitors while conserving server resources.

9.5 Caching Strategies for Performance

Effective caching is a cornerstone of web performance optimization, particularly in environments powered by Nginx. Efficient caching mechanisms reduce server load, decrease response times, and enhance the overall user experience by storing copies of files or dynamically generated pages. This allows subsequent requests for the same content to be served faster, directly from the cache, rather than being processed anew by the server. In this section, we will delve into techniques for configuring and optimizing caching in Nginx to achieve superior performance.

Understanding Nginx Caching Layers

Nginx employs a layered approach to caching, which can be configured both for static and dynamic content. The primary caching layers in Nginx include:

- Browser caching: Instructs the client's browser to store files locally.

- Proxy caching: Nginx acts as a reverse proxy cache, storing responses from a proxied server.

- FastCGI caching: Specifically targets the caching of dynamic content served through FastCGI processors.

Each of these layers can be finely tuned to cache different types of content for varied durations, based on the requirements of the web application.

Configuring Cache Settings in Nginx

Effective cache configuration in Nginx focuses on several directives located within the server or location blocks of the configuration file. Essential directives for caching configuration include:

```
1  proxy_cache_path /path/to/cache levels=1:2 keys_zone=my_cache:10m max_size=1g
       inactive=60m use_temp_path=off;
2
3  server {
4      location / {
5          proxy_cache my_cache;
6          proxy_pass http://my_backend;
7          proxy_cache_key "$scheme$request_method$host$request_uri";
8          proxy_cache_valid 200 302 60m;
```

229

```
 9        proxy_cache_valid 404 1m;
10        add_header X-Cache-Status $upstream_cache_status;
11    }
12 }
```

This example illustrates a basic setup for proxy caching. The `proxy_cache_path` directive defines the path to the cache storage, cache keys zone, the maximum size of the cache, and the inactive time after which cached content is removed.

Maximizing Cache Effectiveness

To maximize the effectiveness of Nginx caching, consider the following strategies:

- Leverage varied cache durations based on content type, using the `proxy_cache_valid` directive to specify how long content should be stored in cache based on the response code.

- Utilize cache keys efficiently by including request elements that uniquely identify a request, ensuring dynamic content is accurately cached and served.

- Implement cache purging mechanisms to maintain cache freshness and relevance, either through manual intervention or by integrating third-party modules that provide automated cache management capabilities.

Monitoring and Debugging Cache Performance

Monitoring cache performance is critical to understanding its impact on web application speed and server load. Nginx provides headers that facilitate the monitoring of cache hits and misses. The `X-Cache-Status` header, added to server responses, indicates whether a request was served from cache (HIT), missed the cache (MISS), or bypassed it (BYPASS).

```
HTTP/1.1 200 OK
```

```
...
X-Cache-Status: HIT
...
```

This output signifies that the request was successfully served from the cache. Regularly monitoring these headers assists in fine-tuning cache settings and identifying patterns that may warrant adjustments to caching strategies.

Implementing and optimizing caching in Nginx significantly contributes to enhancing web performance by reducing server load and improving response times. By understanding the different caching layers available within Nginx, precisely configuring cache settings, utilizing effective caching strategies, and monitoring cache performance, administrators can ensure that web applications are fast, efficient, and scalable. As a result, effective caching becomes an invaluable tool in the arsenal of performance optimization techniques for any Nginx-powered web environment.

9.6   Load Balancing for High Availability and Performance

Load balancing is a fundamental technique in optimizing the distribution of network or application traffic across multiple servers to ensure high availability and performance. In the context of Nginx, load balancing can be effectively utilized to distribute incoming HTTP requests among a pool of backend servers, also known as an upstream group, thereby enhancing the responsiveness and reliability of web applications. This section will discuss the configuration of load balancing in Nginx, types of load balancing methods, and tips for achieving optimal performance and fault tolerance.

Nginx supports various methods of load balancing, including round-robin, least connections, and IP hash. Each method has its advantages and is suited to specific scenarios.

- The round-robin method distributes incoming requests sequentially across the upstream servers. It is the default load balancing method in Nginx and works well in environments where servers are of equivalent specification and load.

- The least connections method forwards the request to the server with the fewest active connections. This method is more efficient than round-robin in scenarios where the request load is unevenly distributed or when the processing time varies significantly among requests.

- The IP hash method routes requests based on the hash of the client's IP address. This ensures that requests from the same client are always directed to the same server, which can be beneficial for session persistence.

To configure load balancing in Nginx, you must define an upstream block in your configuration file. The upstream block specifies the backend servers and the load balancing method.

```
 1  http {
 2      upstream myapp {
 3          least_conn;
 4          server backend1.example.com;
 5          server backend2.example.com;
 6          server backend3.example.com down;
 7      }
 8
 9      server {
10          listen 80;
11
12          location / {
13              proxy_pass http://myapp;
14          }
15      }
16  }
```

In this example, the least_conn method is specified, choosing the server with the fewest active connections for each incoming request. The down parameter indicates that backend3.example.com is temporarily out of service and should not be considered for load balancing.

For high availability and fault tolerance, it is crucial to implement health checks and status monitoring of backend servers. Nginx Plus offers advanced features such as active health checks, which periodically test the availability and responsiveness of backend servers. If a server becomes unresponsive, it is automatically removed from the pool until it recovers, ensuring uninterrupted service.

Load balancing can be further optimized by tuning TCP/IP settings, enabling keepalives, and adjusting timeouts to suit the specific characteristics of your network and applications.

In summary, effective load balancing is pivotal for ensuring high availability and optimal performance of web applications. By carefully selecting the appropriate load balancing method and configuring Nginx correctly, you can achieve a balanced distribution of traffic, minimize response times, and provide a robust and reliable service to your users.

9.7 SSL/TLS Performance Optimization

Optimizing Secure Socket Layer (SSL) and Transport Layer Security (TLS) configurations in Nginx is imperative for enhancing the security and performance of web applications. SSL/TLS protocols are vital for encrypting data transmitted between the client and the server, safeguarding against eavesdropping and man-in-the-middle attacks. However, encryption and decryption processes can impose significant computational overhead, potentially affecting the overall server performance. Focused optimizations can mitigate these overheads, ensuring secure yet efficient data transmission.

The primary step in SSL/TLS performance optimization involves the selection of appropriate cipher suites. Cipher suites dictate the encryption algorithm and key exchange mechanisms used during the SSL/TLS handshake. The choice of cipher suite impacts both the level of security and the computational complexity of the encryption process. Prioritize cipher suites that support forward secrecy and use efficient algorithms such as Elliptic Curve Cryptography (ECC), which offers the same level of security as RSA with shorter key lengths, thus reducing computational effort.

To configure preferred cipher suites in Nginx, modify the ssl_ciphers directive within the server configuration block. An optimal configuration may look as follows:

```
1   ssl_ciphers 'ECDHE-ECDSA-AES128-GCM-SHA256:
2               ECDHE-RSA-AES128-GCM-SHA256:
3               ECDHE-ECDSA-AES256-GCM-SHA384:
4               ECDHE-RSA-AES256-GCM-SHA384:
5               DHE-RSA-AES128-GCM-SHA256:
6               DHE-DSS-AES128-GCM-SHA256';
```

Furthermore, enabling SSL session caching can substantially reduce the SSL/TLS handshake time for subsequent connections. SSL session caching allows the server and client to reuse previously negotiated parameters, obviating the need for a full handshake. Configure SSL session caching in Nginx using the ssl_session_cache directive:

```
1   ssl_session_cache shared:SSL:10m;
2   ssl_session_timeout 10m;
```

This configuration allocates 10MB of shared memory for storing SSL session parameters and sets the cache expiration time to 10 minutes. Adjust these values based on the traffic patterns and requirements of your web application.

Enabling OpenSSL's built-in hardware acceleration feature can also optimize SSL/TLS processing. This feature leverages the cryptographic capabilities of modern processors, further reducing encryption and decryption overheads. Although Nginx automatically benefits from OpenSSL's acceleration when available, verify that Nginx and OpenSSL are compiled with hardware acceleration support.

Integrating SSL/TLS performance optimization into your Nginx configuration enhances both security and user experience. By carefully selecting cipher suites, enabling SSL session caching, and utilizing hardware acceleration, web administrators can ensure efficient and secure data transmission, catering to the demands of contemporary web applications.

9.8 Leveraging HTTP/2 for Improved Performance

HTTP/2 represents a significant evolution over its predecessor, HTTP/1.1, introducing optimizations that greatly enhance web performance. The primary goal of HTTP/2 is to reduce latency by enabling full request and response multiplexing, effectively allowing multiple requests to be sent over a single TCP connection simultaneously. This paradigm shift addresses the head-of-line blocking problem inherent to HTTP/1.1, where requests are processed in the order received, causing delays.

Enabling HTTP/2 in Nginx

To utilize HTTP/2 in Nginx, it's essential to first ensure that the Nginx version in use supports HTTP/2. This can be confirmed by checking the version using the command nginx -v. Versions 1.9.5 and above come with HTTP/2 support. Enabling HTTP/2 in Nginx is straightforward and involves updating the server block configuration to include the http2 parameter in the listen directive as shown below:

```
1  server {
2      listen 443 ssl http2;
3      server_name your_domain.com;
4
5      ssl_certificate /path/to/your/certificate.pem;
6      ssl_certificate_key /path/to/your/private.key;
7
8      # Other configurations...
9  }
```

No additional modules are required to enable HTTP/2, but it's important to note that HTTP/2 over Nginx requires an SSL/TLS certificate as it operates exclusively over HTTPS for security reasons.

HTTP/2 Performance Features

HTTP/2 introduces several key features aimed at improving performance, notably:

- **Multiplexing:** Multiple requests and responses can be in flight simultaneously over a single TCP connection, significantly reducing latency.

- **Server Push:** Allows a server to send resources to a client proactively before they are explicitly requested, improving load times.

- **Header Compression:** HTTP/2 employs HPACK compression for HTTP headers, reducing overhead.

- **Stream Prioritization:** Resources can be assigned priority levels, enabling browsers to load critical resources first.

These features collectively contribute to more efficient use of underlying TCP connections, reduced latency, and improved loading times of web assets.

Optimizing Nginx for HTTP/2

While enabling HTTP/2 in Nginx offers immediate performance gains, further optimizations can be achieved through tuning specific directives:

- **ssl_buffer_size:** Adjusting the SSL buffer size can influence throughput and latency. For HTTP/2, a smaller buffer size around 4k or 8k can improve performance as it results in quicker transmission of data frames.

- **ssl_session_cache:** Enabling SSL session caching reduces the SSL/TLS handshake overhead for subsequent connections, speeding up encrypted content delivery.

Implementing these adjustments involves adding or modifying directives in the Nginx configuration file, within the server block for your site:

```
1  ssl_buffer_size 4k;
2  ssl_session_cache shared:SSL:10m;
```

Monitoring the performance impact of these changes is crucial. Tools such as WebPageTest or Chrome's DevTools Network panel can provide insights into HTTP/2 performance characteristics and help identify areas for further optimization.

Leveraging HTTP/2 in Nginx stands as a potent means to enhance web application performance. Through multiplexing, server push, and other innovations, HTTP/2 addresses the limiting factors of HTTP/1.1. By enabling HTTP/2 and applying targeted optimizations within Nginx configurations, web administrators can realize substantial improvements in speed, efficiency, and user experience. Leveraging HTTP/2 for Improved Performance

9.9 Fine-Tuning Worker Processes and Connections

Fine-tuning the number of worker processes and their connection limits is paramount in optimizing Nginx for better performance. The worker_processes directive in the Nginx configuration file determines how many worker processes will be created. Ideally, this should be equal to the number of CPU cores available on the server to ensure efficient load distribution and to utilize the hardware optimally.

To identify the optimal number of worker_processes, it's recommended to consider the architecture of the server and its expected load. For instance, on a server with 4 CPU cores, setting worker_processes to 4 would typically yield the best performance under most conditions.

```
1  worker_processes auto;
```

The directive above configures Nginx to automatically determine the optimal number of worker processes based on the available CPU cores. This is particularly useful for servers where the hardware may change or be updated frequently.

In addition to the `worker_processes`, configuring the right number of worker connections is critical. The `worker_connections` directive specifies the maximum number of connections that each worker process can handle. The total capacity of the server to handle concurrent connections can be calculated by the formula:

$$\text{Total\_Connections} = \text{worker\_processes} \times \text{worker\_connections} \quad (9.1)$$

It's important to ensure the `worker_connections` value is set within the limits of the operating system's maximum allowed file descriptors. This can be viewed and adjusted using the `ulimit` command in most Unix-based systems.

```
1   worker_connections 1024;
```

For intensive workloads or applications that require long-polling or WebSocket connections, increasing `worker_connections` is necessary. However, every increase should be carefully considered, as setting this value too high can lead to unnecessary resource consumption and potentially degrade system performance.

After adjusting `worker_processes` and `worker_connections`, monitoring and tuning are ongoing processes. Using real-time monitoring tools to observe the server's performance under different loads can help in identifying bottlenecks or the need for further adjustments.

In summary, the proper configuration of worker processes and connections plays a critical role in Nginx's performance. By leveraging the server's hardware effectively and monitoring performance closely, administrators can ensure that their Nginx servers are optimized for handling high traffic volumes efficiently.

9.10 Monitoring System Resources for Bottlenecks

In this section, we will discuss the importance of systematically monitoring system resources to identify potential bottlenecks that may hinder the performance of Nginx. Identifying these bottlenecks early allows for targeted optimization efforts, ensuring that web services remain efficient and responsive under varying loads.

First, it is crucial to understand the types of resources that should be monitored:

- CPU usage - High CPU usage can indicate an excessive load or inefficient processing.

- Memory utilization - Memory leaks or insufficient memory can lead to swapping, severely degrading performance.

- Disk I/O - High disk I/O can be a bottleneck for content delivery, especially for dynamic content.

- Network bandwidth - Insufficient bandwidth can limit the capacity to serve content to users.

Monitoring tools play a critical role in gathering data on these resources. Popular choices include `top`, `htop`, `iotop`, and `iftop` for real-time system monitoring, while tools like `vmstat`, `iostat`, and `sar` offer more comprehensive data collection capabilities. Additionally, specific tools like `nginx-status` module provide metrics directly related to Nginx's performance.

A typical pattern to identify bottlenecks involves collecting and analyzing usage statistics over time. For instance, using `iostat` with the following command:

```
iostat -x 1
```

This command provides extended statistics updated every second, allowing administrators to observe disk I/O performance in real-time. Anomalies in read/write speeds or unusually high I/O wait times can signal disk-related bottlenecks.

Similarly, monitoring network bandwidth with `iftop` can reveal bandwidth limitations. By executing the command:

```
1   iftop
```

Administrators can observe incoming and outgoing traffic volumes, spotting potential network congestion issues.

To diagnose CPU-related performance issues, one might use `htop`, which provides a dynamic overview of system processes and their CPU usage. Higher than expected CPU usage for the Nginx process could indicate inefficient configuration or the need for more hardware resources.

In terms of memory utilization, tools like `vmstat` can offer insights into memory swapping activities, which significantly impact performance. By checking the swap in (`si`) and swap out (`so`) columns, administrators can gauge if memory capacity is adequate.

```
1   vmstat 1
```

Finally, implementing comprehensive monitoring using advanced tools like `Prometheus` and `Grafana` can offer a more holistic view. These tools allow for the creation of dashboards that document the health of the system over time, making it easier to predict future bottlenecks and proactively adjust configurations.

To conclude, effective monitoring of system resources is paramount in identifying and resolving bottlenecks in Nginx server environments. By employing a combination of monitoring tools and techniques, administrators can ensure optimal performance and reliability of their web services.

9.11   Advanced Performance Tools and Techniques

To enhance the performance of Nginx further, leveraging advanced performance tools and techniques can provide deeper insights into the web server's behavior and help pinpoint areas for optimization. This section discusses some sophisticated tools and methodologies that can be deployed to monitor performance, analyze traffic, and optimize Nginx configurations for peak efficiency.

Using   Ngx_http_stub_status_module   for   Real-time Metrics

One of the first steps in performance tuning is to gather accurate and timely data about the web server's operation.   The ngx_http_stub_status_module of Nginx provides critical real-time metrics about the server, including the number of active connections, the number of requests per connection, and the total number of handled requests.

To enable this module, the following configuration needs to be added to the Nginx configuration file:

```
1  location /nginx_status {
2      stub_status on;
3      access_log off;
4      allow 127.0.0.1;
5      deny all;
6  }
```

Accessing the /nginx_status URL will display metrics in a plain-text format, ideal for parsing by external monitoring tools. Reading and analyzing these metrics regularly aids in understanding traffic patterns and identifying bottlenecks.

Profiling with Google PageSpeed Module

Optimizing content delivery is critical for improving web performance. The PageSpeed module by Google, integrated within Nginx, automates several optimization techniques, including minification of CSS, JavaScript, and HTML, optimizing images by resizing and compression, and reordering CSS and JavaScript for optimal rendering.

The configuration to integrate Google PageSpeed with Nginx is as follows:

```
1  pagespeed on;
2  pagespeed FileCachePath /var/ngx_pagespeed_cache;
3  location ~ "\.pagespeed\.([a-z]\.)?[a-z]{2}\.[^.]{10}\.[^.]+" { add_header "" ""
     ; }
4  location ~ "^/ngx_pagespeed_static/" { }
5  location ~ "^/ngx_pagespeed_beacon$" { }
```

Implementing PageSpeed can substantially decrease page load times by reducing the size of resources and optimizing their delivery.

Tuning with ngx_http_gzip_module for Content Compression

Compression is another vital technique to improve the performance of web applications. The ngx_http_gzip_module enables gzip compression for specified MIME types, which can drastically reduce the amount of data transmitted over the network.

The basic setup for enabling gzip compression is:

```
1  gzip on;
2  gzip_types text/plain application/xml application/json;
3  gzip_min_length 1000;
```

This configuration enables gzip compression for plain text, XML, and JSON content types, only compressing responses larger than 1000 bytes to avoid the overhead of compressing small resources.

Leveraging Nginx Plus for Advanced Monitoring and Management

Nginx Plus, the commercial edition of Nginx, provides advanced monitoring and management capabilities through a real-time dashboard. It offers insights into HTTP and TCP/UDP traffic, server health, and performance metrics, enabling administrators to make informed decisions regarding scaling and optimization.

Furthermore, Nginx Plus supports session persistence, adaptive media streaming, and advanced load balancing algorithms, making it a powerful tool for ensuring high availability and performance of web applications.

By integrating advanced tools and techniques such as ngx_http_stub_status_module, Google PageSpeed, ngx_http_gzip_module, and leveraging the enhanced capabilities of Nginx Plus, administrators can significantly fine-tune the performance of their web services. Regular analysis and optimization based on the metrics gathered from these tools ensure that Nginx runs efficiently, handles high traffic volumes with minimal latency, and delivers content rapidly to end-users, offering an optimized web experience.

Chapter 10

Advanced Nginx Features and Module Development

Exploring advanced Nginx features and engaging in module development allows for the customization and extension of Nginx's capabilities beyond its core functionality. Advanced features, such as dynamic module loading, stream processing, and the embedding of programming languages directly within Nginx, open up new possibilities for high-performance web applications. Additionally, developers can create custom modules to introduce specific functionalities tailored to their unique requirements. This aspect of Nginx not only enhances its adaptability and efficiency in handling diverse web serving and proxying tasks but also fosters a vibrant community contributing to its ecosystem, ensuring Nginx remains at the forefront of web server technology.

10.1   Exploring Advanced Nginx Features

Advanced Nginx features significantly enhance its functionality, enabling it to meet complex web serving and proxying requirements. This section will discuss several of these features, including dynamic module loading, stream processing, embedded programming languages, secure links, and the use of Nginx as a mail proxy.

Dynamic Module Loading

Dynamic module loading allows administrators to add or remove Nginx modules without recompiling the entire server. Previously, introducing new functionality or updates necessitated a server rebuild. However, with dynamic loading, modules can be managed more flexibly, akin to plug-and-play components.

To enable a module dynamically, include the `load_module` directive in the Nginx configuration file, specifying the path to the module's shared object (.so) file. For example:

```
1  load_module modules/ngx_http_geoip_module.so;
```

This directive loads the GeoIP module, enabling geo-targeting features.

Stream Processing

Stream processing is another advanced feature facilitating the handling of arbitrary TCP and UDP traffic. It supports load balancing, allowing Nginx to distribute incoming data streams across multiple backend servers based on configured routing algorithms.

Configuring stream processing involves defining a `stream` block in the Nginx configuration. Inside this block, you can specify server groups and routing methods. Here is a basic example that sets up stream forwarding:

```
1  stream {
2      upstream backend {
3          server backend1.example.com:12345;
4          server backend2.example.com:12345;
5      }
6
7      server {
```

```
 8       listen 12345;
 9       proxy_pass backend;
10    }
11 }
```

Embedding Programming Languages

Nginx can also embed programming languages, like Lua, directly within its configuration, allowing for highly dynamic and customizable content handling. The `ngx_http_lua_module` module adds Lua support, enabling scripts to run at various phases of the request processing cycle.

Here's how to define a Lua content handler:

```
1 location /lua_content {
2     content_by_lua_block {
3         ngx.say("Hello from Lua!")
4     }
5 }
```

This configuration makes Nginx serve the string "Hello from Lua!" whenever the '/lua_content' location is accessed.

Secure Links

The Secure Links module provides a method to protect resources with a hash-based access control mechanism. It ensures that a link is only accessible if the requester has the correct token, which is typically generated on-the-fly and expires after a predetermined period.

To utilize Secure Links, define a location with the `secure_link` and `secure_link_md5` directives:

```
1 location /protected {
2     secure_link $arg_md5,$arg_expires;
3     secure_link_md5 "secret$uri$arg_expires";
4
5     if ($secure_link = "") {
6         return 403;
7     }
8
```

```
9     if ($secure_link = "0") {
10        return 410;
11    }
12 }
```

This configuration secures the '/protected' location, requiring a valid MD5 hash and expiration timestamp as request parameters.

Mail Proxy

Nginx can function as a mail proxy server, handling IMAP, SMTP, and POP3 protocols. This capability allows it to provide authentication and routing for mail services, integrating seamlessly with existing email infrastructure.

Setting up Nginx as a mail proxy involves configuring a `mail` block in the Nginx configuration file. Within this block, specify the mail protocols to be proxied and the backend servers handling the actual mail services.

```
1 mail {
2     server_name mail.example.com;
3     auth_http localhost/auth;
4
5     imap_backend imap.example.com:143;
6     smtp_backend smtp.example.com:25;
7     pop3_backend pop3.example.com:110;
8 }
```

This basic setup configures Nginx to authenticate mail clients and route their requests to the appropriate backend servers based on the protocol being used.

In summary, exploring these advanced Nginx features unveils the server's capacity to handle a broad spectrum of web and mail serving scenarios, providing developers and administrators with powerful tools to tailor their services to specific needs.

10.2 Introduction to Nginx Module Development

Nginx module development stands as a pivotal extension mechanism allowing for immense customization of Nginx's functionality. Modules enable the introduction of specific features that are not part of the core Nginx distribution, enhancing its capability as a web server and a reverse proxy.

To understand Nginx module development, it is essential to grasp the architecture of Nginx itself. Nginx is designed around an event-driven architecture, making it highly efficient at handling concurrent connections. This is one of the primary reasons for its widespread adoption for high-traffic websites. Modules developed for Nginx must adhere to this architectural principle to maintain efficiency and performance.

There are two primary types of modules in Nginx: core modules and third-party modules. Core modules are included in the Nginx source distribution and cover fundamental functionalities such as HTTP processing, mail proxy, and stream processing. Third-party modules, on the other hand, are developed by the community and can be dynamically loaded into Nginx. This flexibility allows developers to extend Nginx in various directions, including but not limited to security enhancements, sophisticated load balancing algorithms, or integration with external systems.

The development of a Nginx module typically follows these steps:

- Identifying the need or functionality gap that the module will address.

- Setting up a development environment for Nginx and module compilation.

- Familiarizing oneself with Nginx's internal APIs and the module development process.

- Writing the module code, adhering to Nginx's coding standards and architectural principles.

- Testing the module extensively to ensure it works as intended and does not introduce regressions to Nginx's performance or stability.

- Packaging the module for distribution and use with Nginx.

A crucial aspect of developing modules for Nginx is understanding its internal APIs. Nginx exposes a set of hooks and directives that modules can leverage. These APIs allow modules to interact with the request processing pipeline, manipulate request and response headers, manage configuration directives, and more. Familiarity with Nginx's processing phases and how modules can hook into these phases is fundamental for effective module development.

Modules can be classified based on the functionality they provide and the phase of request processing they operate on. Some modules might be involved in the early stages of request processing, such as parsing request headers, while others may deal with content generation or filtering response data.

Developing a Nginx module requires a combination of C programming skills and a deep understanding of Nginx's architecture. The process can be challenging but ultimately rewarding, as it allows for significant customization and optimization of web server operations. The vibrant Nginx community actively supports module development, offering resources, documentation, and forums for discussion and collaboration.

Nginx module development is a powerful mechanism for extending the capabilities of Nginx. Whether aiming to introduce new functionalities, enhance existing features, or integrate with external systems, module development allows developers to tailor Nginx to their specific needs, contributing to its popularity and effectiveness as a web server and reverse proxy solution.

10.3   Types of Modules in Nginx

Nginx, well-regarded for its versatility and high performance as a web server, owes much of its flexibility to its modular architecture. This architecture enables Nginx to be extended with additional capabilities through the use of modules. There are several types of modules in Nginx, each designed to perform specific functions within the web server's environment.   Understanding these modules is crucial for anyone looking to develop for Nginx or to customize it for specific web serving or proxying tasks.

Core Modules

Core modules are integral to Nginx, providing the essential functionalities that the web server requires to operate effectively. These modules include:

- The `http_core` module, which handles basic HTTP functionality.

- The `events_core` module, responsible for managing the event-driven model that Nginx uses for handling connections.

- The `errlog_module`, which is used for logging error messages.

These core modules are compiled into Nginx by default and are necessary for its operation.

Standard HTTP Modules

Standard HTTP modules extend Nginx's capabilities in handling HTTP requests. They include functionalities such as:

- Authentication and authorization, with modules like `auth_basic_module` and `auth_request_module`.

- Content modification before serving to the client, through modules like `subs_filter_module` and `addition_module`.

- Data compression, specifically with the `gzip_module`, which allows for the compression of HTTP responses.

These modules are usually included with a standard Nginx installation but may be enabled or disabled based on the build options.

Mail Modules

Mail modules provide support for proxying and authentication for mail protocols (SMTP, IMAP, POP3). The primary module responsible for these tasks is the `mail_core_module`. It leverages other, more specific modules like `smtp_module`, `imap_module`, and `pop3_module` to handle the respective protocols.

Third-Party Modules

The vibrant Nginx community has created a wide array of third-party modules that introduce new features or enhance existing ones. Examples include:

- `ngx_pagespeed`, which optimizes site performance by reworking web pages and assets.

- `mod_security`, an open-source Web Application Firewall (WAF) that provides various security features.

Integrating these modules requires compiling them with the Nginx source code, as they are not included by default.

Dynamic Modules

With the introduction of dynamic module support in Nginx 1.9.11, it became possible to load modules at runtime without needing to recompile Nginx. This advancement greatly simplifies the process of extending Nginx's capabilities. To load a dynamic module, use the load_module directive in the Nginx configuration file, specifying the path to the dynamic module's shared object file.

Understanding the types of modules in Nginx and how they contribute to the web server's functionality allows developers and administrators to tailor the server to their specific requirements. Whether by using the core and standard modules included with Nginx, integrating third-party modules, or developing custom modules, one can enhance and customize the functionality of Nginx to meet the unique demands of any web serving or proxying task.

10.4 Setting Up Development Environment for Module Development

Setting up a proper development environment is a critical step in Nginx module development. It not only facilitates a streamlined workflow but also ensures that the developed modules are compatible and perform optimally with the Nginx core. This section will delineate the steps and requirements for configuring an effective development setting.

Before delving into the specific steps, it is important to highlight that module development for Nginx necessitates a solid understanding of C programming language, as Nginx modules are predominantly written in C. Additionally, familiarity with the build and configuration processes of Nginx itself is beneficial.

- **Installing Necessary Tools and Libraries:** The first step involves installing the compiler tools and libraries required for building Nginx from source, as well as for developing and compiling your custom modules. On a Debian-based system, you can install these using the following command:

```
1   $ sudo apt-get install build-essential libpcre3 libpcre3-dev zlib1g
        zlib1g-dev libssl-dev
```

- **Downloading Nginx Source Code:** To develop modules compatible with a specific Nginx version, you should download the corresponding source code of Nginx. This ensures that the module integrates smoothly with the Nginx core. You can download the source code from the official Nginx website or via wget:

```
1  $ wget http://nginx.org/download/nginx-1.18.0.tar.gz
2  $ tar zxvf nginx-1.18.0.tar.gz
```

  Replace "1.18.0" with the version number for which you wish to develop your module.

- **Exploring the Nginx Source Code:** Prior to commencing module development, it's important to familiarize yourself with the structure and make-up of the Nginx source code. This includes understanding the directory structure, core modules, and build configuration files. Familiarity with Nginx internals can greatly aid in module development.

- **Setting Up the Development Environment:** For coding, any text editor or integrated development environment (IDE) that supports C programming can be utilized. However, some IDEs offer features like code completion, syntax highlighting, and debugging tools tailored for Nginx module development. Configuring your environment with tools like gcc for compiling and make for automated builds is essential.

- **Configuring Build System for Module Development:** To compile your module with Nginx, you need to add your module to the Nginx build configuration. This involves modifying the ./configure script arguments to include your module by using the --add-module option:

```
1  $ ./configure --add-module=/path/to/your/module
2  $ make
3  $ sudo make install
```

  This process compiles Nginx with your module included, making it ready for testing and further development.

- **Regularly Updating Your Development Environment:** Nginx is actively developed, and new versions are frequently released. Keeping your development environment up to date with the latest version of the Nginx source code is crucial for ensuring compatibility and taking advantage of the latest features and improvements in your module development efforts.

In summary, setting up a development environment for Nginx module development involves installing the necessary tools and libraries, downloading the Nginx source code, familiarizing yourself with its structure, setting up your IDE or text editor, and configuring the build system to include your module. Following these steps will ensure a fruitful and effective module development process.

10.5   Creating a Basic Nginx Module

Creating a basic Nginx module requires an understanding of the structure and building blocks of an Nginx module. Modules in Nginx are designed to extend its capabilities, allowing it to handle additional tasks or process requests in specific ways. This section will guide you through the steps involved in creating a simple Nginx module from scratch.

Module Structure

An Nginx module typically consists of several key components:

- A `config` file that instructs the Nginx build system how to compile the module.

- A source file (`.c`) that contains the implementation of the module.

- An optional header file (`.h`) that declares the functions and variables used across the module.

Setting Up the Development Environment

Before delving into the module creation process, ensure your development environment is ready. This involves having Nginx installed either from the source or through a package manager and having access to a C compiler like gcc.

Creating the Config File

The first step in creating a new Nginx module is to write a `config` file. This file informs the Nginx build system about your module, its source files, and any additional compilation flags that may be necessary. A simple `config` file might look something like this:

```
1  ngx_addon_name=ngx_http_my_module
2  HTTP_MODULES="$HTTP_MODULES ngx_http_my_module"
3  NGX_ADDON_SRCS="$NGX_ADDON_SRCS $ngx_addon_dir/ngx_http_my_module.c"
```

This script sets the module name and adds the module's source file to the build configuration.

Implementing the Module

Module implementation involves writing the C code that defines the module's functionality. At a minimum, an Nginx module must define a module context and a module directives array.

```
1  #include <ngx_config.h>
2  #include <ngx_core.h>
3  #include <ngx_http.h>
4
5  static ngx_command_t ngx_http_my_module_commands[] = {
6      { ngx_string("my_directive"),
7        NGX_HTTP_MAIN_CONF|NGX_CONF_NOARGS,
8        ngx_http_my_module_handler,
9        0,
10       0,
11       NULL },
12
13       ngx_null_command
14  };
15
16  static ngx_http_module_t ngx_http_my_module_ctx = {
17      NULL, /* preconfiguration */
```

```
18      NULL, /* postconfiguration */
19      NULL, /* create main configuration */
20      NULL, /* init main configuration */
21      NULL, /* create server configuration */
22      NULL, /* merge server configuration */
23      NULL, /* create location configuration */
24      NULL, /* merge location configuration */
25    };
26
27    ngx_module_t ngx_http_my_module = {
28      NGX_MODULE_V1,
29      &ngx_http_my_module_ctx, /* module context */
30      ngx_http_my_module_commands, /* module directives */
31      NGX_HTTP_MODULE, /* module type */
32      NULL, /* init master */
33      NULL, /* init module */
34      NULL, /* init process */
35      NULL, /* init thread */
36      NULL, /* exit thread */
37      NULL, /* exit process */
38      NULL, /* exit master */
39      NGX_MODULE_V1_PADDING
40    };
```

In this example, `ngx_http_my_module_commands` defines a module directive named `my_directive` and its handler function. The module context `ngx_http_my_module_ctx` and the module definition `ngx_http_my_module` are also specified.

Compiling the Module

To compile the module, you must rebuild Nginx from source, including the module's `config` file in the process. The general steps include configuring Nginx with the `--add-module` option pointing to your module's directory, compiling, and installing Nginx.

```
./configure --add-module=/path/to/your/module
make
sudo make install
```

After installation, you can start using the module by including its directives in the Nginx configuration files.

Creating a basic Nginx module involves setting up a development environment, writing a `config` file, implementing the module in C, and compiling Nginx with the module included. This process allows

developers to extend Nginx's functionality to meet specific requirements, making it an extremely flexible web server solution.

10.6   Understanding Nginx's Internal APIs

Nginx's internal APIs offer a robust framework for module
developers, facilitating the creation of efficient and powerful
modules. These APIs enable interaction with core functionalities of
Nginx, allowing developers to manipulate request handling,
configure directives, manage content delivery, and utilize utility
functions for common operations. A comprehensive understanding
of these APIs is essential for leveraging Nginx's capabilities to their
full extent.

The Nginx API is organized into several core components, each
serving a distinct purpose within the infrastructure of an Nginx
module. These components are not standalone libraries but are
intertwined within the Nginx architecture, providing a seamless
interface for module development.

- **Request Handling:** At the heart of Nginx's functionality is its
  ability to efficiently process and respond to HTTP requests.
  The request handling API provides a multitude of functions to
  interact with the request/response cycle. Developers can use
  these functions to read or modify headers, process request
  bodies, and control the flow of request handling.

```
1   ngx_http_request_t *r; // Represents an HTTP request
2   ngx_http_read_client_request_body(r, callback);
```

- **Configuration and Directive Processing:** Nginx modules often
  expose configuration directives to be used within Nginx config
  files. The configuration API allows modules to define, parse,
  and use these directives. Additionally, it provides mechanisms
  for merging configuration values between different scopes.

- **Content Generation:** Modules that generate or manipulate
  content, such as filters or content providers, rely on the

content generation API. This API includes functions for sending headers, outputting body content, and managing request buffers.

```
1  ngx_int_t ngx_http_send_header(ngx_http_request_t *r);
2  ngx_int_t ngx_http_output_filter(ngx_http_request_t *r, ngx_chain_t *
       chain);
```

- **Utility Functions:** Beyond request handling and content management, the Nginx API offers a wide array of utility functions. These cover tasks such as logging, memory management, time retrieval, and string manipulation.

```
1  ngx_log_error(NGX_LOG_ERR, r->connection->log, 0, "Error message");
2  void *p = ngx_palloc(r->pool, sizeof(my_struct));
```

A pivotal aspect of module development is interfacing with Nginx's processing phases via its APIs. Nginx processes a request in several phases, including the post-read phase, server rewrite phase, location rewrite phase, access phase, content generation phase, and log phase. By hooking into these phases, modules can execute their functions at the appropriate point in the request life cycle.

```
HTTP request received -> Post-read phase -> Server rewrite phase
-> Find config location -> Location rewrite phase -> Access phase
-> Try files -> Content generation phase -> Log phase
```

Understanding when and how to hook into these phases is critical for module effectiveness and performance. For instance, a module aiming to modify request headers would logically insert its processing in the pre-access phase.

Nginx's internal APIs provide a comprehensive and powerful toolset for module development, offering versatility and control over web server functionality. Familiarity with these APIs and strategic integration into Nginx's processing phases are crucial for developing modules that are both effective and efficient.

10.7   Hooking into Nginx's Processing Phases

Nginx processing of requests is a phased operation, enabling
fine-grained control over how requests are handled. Each phase in
the request lifecycle offers a hook, allowing modules to interact
with the request at designated points.   Understanding how to
effectively integrate custom logic into these phases is paramount for
module developers looking to extend Nginx's capabilities.   This
section will delve into the intricacies of hooking custom modules
into Nginx's processing phases, providing a scaffold for developers
to build more complex and tailored web solutions.

The   key   to   successful   module   development   lies   in   the
comprehension of how and when to attach custom processing logic
to these phases. Nginx defines a series of processing phases such as
the rewrite phase, access phase, content phase, among others.
Each phase serves a specific purpose in the request processing
pipeline, offering a unique opportunity for intervention.

To illustrate the process of hooking into these phases, consider a module that logs detailed request processing metrics. For this purpose,
the log_phase_handler can be used. Below is a skeletal example that
demonstrates the registration of a handler in the post-access phase:

```
static ngx_int_t ngx_http_custom_module_init(ngx_conf_t *cf) {
    ngx_http_core_main_conf_t *cmcf;
    cmcf = ngx_http_conf_get_module_main_conf(cf, ngx_http_core_module);

    ngx_http_handler_pt *h;
    h = ngx_array_push(&cmcf->phases[NGX_HTTP_LOG_PHASE].handlers);
    if (h == NULL) {
        return NGX_ERROR;
    }

    *h = ngx_http_custom_log_handler;

    return NGX_OK;
}

static ngx_int_t ngx_http_custom_log_handler(ngx_http_request_t *r) {
    // Custom processing logic here
    // For instance, log request timings or specific headers

    return NGX_OK;
}
```

In the given example, the function `ngx_http_custom_module_init` is responsible for initializing the module and hooking the custom log handler into the LOG phase. The `ngx_http_custom_log_handler` function defines the logic to be executed during this phase. It's worth noting that each handler must return a status code, indicating the outcome of its execution. The NGX_OK return value signifies successful completion, allowing Nginx to proceed to the next phase or operation.

When developing modules, understanding the order and implications of the processing phases is crucial. Improperly hooking into a phase or returning incorrect status codes from handlers can lead to unintended behavior or processing errors. Therefore, developers must design their module logic with careful consideration of how it integrates into the existing Nginx processing pipeline.

Leveraging these hooks, developers can significantly extend and customize Nginx's functionality. Whether it's adding custom logging, modifying request handlers, enhancing security measures, or integrating new content generation methods, the ability to hook into the processing phases provides a powerful toolset for creating highly efficient and tailored web serving solutions.

Hooking into Nginx's processing phases is a central technique in Nginx module development. It allows developers to insert custom logic precisely where it's needed in the request handling process. By carefully selecting the appropriate phase and implementing the handler logic accordingly, developers can achieve sophisticated custom behaviors, greatly enhancing Nginx's utility and performance for specific tasks or applications.

10.8   Config Directives for Custom Modules

Configuring Nginx involves directives specified in the configuration file. These directives are essential for the customization and control over Nginx's behavior. When developing custom modules, defining and handling configuration directives is crucial for integrating the module's functionality with the Nginx configuration system. This section delves into the implementation process of config directives for custom modules, including directive declaration, parsing, and usage within a module.

Firstly, let's discuss how to declare configuration directives for a custom module. Directives in Nginx are declared in the ngx_command_t structure. Each directive your module will support must have an entry in this structure. A basic declaration involves specifying the name of the directive, its type, the function that will handle the directive, the configuration structure where the directive's value will be stored, and the configuration phase during which the directive is valid.

For illustration, consider the following code snippet that declares a simple directive:

```
static ngx_command_t my_module_commands[] = {
    {
      ngx_string("my_directive"),
      NGX_HTTP_MAIN_CONF|NGX_CONF_TAKE1,
      ngx_conf_set_str_slot,
      NGX_HTTP_LOC_CONF_OFFSET,
      offsetof(my_loc_conf, my_directive_value),
      NULL
    },

    ngx_null_command
};
```

In this snippet, the directive my_directive is designed to take one argument (NGX_CONF_TAKE1) and store it in the my_loc_conf structure. The ngx_conf_set_str_slot is a generic handler provided by Nginx for setting a string value in the configuration.

Next, let's move to parsing directives. When Nginx processes the configuration file, it calls the handler function associated with each directive it encounters. The handler function must adhere to a specific prototype defined by Nginx. For string-type directives, a common handler like ngx_conf_set_str_slot can be used, which simplifies parsing.

To illustrate how a custom directive can be used within a module, consider the following example where a module performs an operation based on the value of my_directive:

```
static ngx_int_t my_module_handler(ngx_http_request_t *r) {
  my_loc_conf_t *conf;

  conf = ngx_http_get_module_loc_conf(r, my_module);

  if (conf->my_directive_value != NULL) {
    ngx_log_error(NGX_LOG_NOTICE, r->connection->log, 0,
              "my_directive is: %s", conf->my_directive_value->data);
  }

  return NGX_OK;
}
```

When handling a request, this code checks if the my_directive has been set and logs its value. This example demonstrates how a module can access and utilize the configuration parameters defined by its directives.

Finally, it is important to mention the inclusion of the directive in the module's context. Nginx modules must define a module context (ngx_module_t) that, among other things, includes the module's commands array:

```
static ngx_http_module_t my_module_ctx = {
  NULL, /* preconfiguration */
  NULL, /* postconfiguration */

  NULL, /* create main configuration */
  NULL, /* init main configuration */

  NULL, /* create server configuration */
  NULL, /* merge server configuration */

  create_my_loc_conf, /* create location configuration */
  merge_my_loc_conf /* merge location configuration */
};

ngx_module_t my_module = {
  NGX_MODULE_V1,
  &my_module_ctx, /* module context */
  my_module_commands, /* module directives */
  NGX_HTTP_MODULE, /* module type */
  NULL, /* init master */
  NULL, /* init module */
  NULL, /* init process */
  NULL, /* init thread */
  NULL, /* exit thread */
  NULL, /* exit process */
  NULL, /* exit master */
  NGX_MODULE_V1_PADDING
```

```
28  };
```

This section illustrated how custom configuration directives are a powerful mechanism for extending Nginx's functionality through modules.   By adhering to the process of directive declaration, parsing, and usage within a module, developers can effectively leverage Nginx's extensibility to accommodate a wide range of web serving and proxying scenarios.

10.9   Debugging and Testing Nginx Modules

Debugging and testing are critical phases in the development lifecycle of Nginx modules. Given the nature of web servers operating in multi-threaded environments, issues such as race conditions, memory leaks, and deadlocks can be particularly challenging to identify and fix. These processes ensure that modules function correctly under various conditions and adhere to expected performance benchmarks.

Preparation for Debugging

Before delving into debugging strategies, it is imperative to set up an appropriate environment that facilitates the identification and resolution of bugs. This setup involves compiling Nginx with debugging symbols and enabling the debugging logs.

To compile Nginx with debugging symbols, the --with-debug option must be included during the configuration step. This option ensures that the resultant binary contains additional debugging information, which is invaluable when stepping through code during troubleshooting.

```
1  ./configure --with-debug
2  make
3  sudo make install
```

Enabling debugging logs in Nginx involves modifying the

nginx.conf configuration file. Specifically, the error_log directive must be set to the debug level.

```
1  error_log /var/log/nginx/error.log debug;
```

These logs will provide verbose output about Nginx's activities, including the handling of client requests, execution of specific handler functions, and internal state changes, offering valuable insights when diagnosing issues.

Strategies for Debugging

Once the environment is configured for enhanced logging and debug information, several strategies can be employed to identify and resolve bugs within Nginx modules.

Analyzing Debug Logs

The debug logs generated by Nginx can be overwhelming due to their verbosity. It is crucial to understand the structure of these logs and to filter them effectively to isolate relevant entries. Tools such as grep, awk, or even custom scripts can be helpful in parsing and analyzing log files.

Using a Debugger

A debugger, such as GDB, can attach to the running Nginx process, providing the ability to set breakpoints, step through code, and inspect the state of program variables at runtime. This interactive approach is particularly useful for investigating complex issues that are not easily revealed through static analysis or log file review.

```
1  gdb /usr/sbin/nginx
```

Testing Frameworks

Automated testing frameworks, such as Test::Nginx, offer a structured approach to validate the behavior of Nginx modules under various scenarios. Writing comprehensive test cases that cover the expected functionality and edge cases can help identify bugs early in the development process.

```
1  use Test::Nginx::Socket;
2  run_tests();
```

Common Debugging Scenarios

Several common scenarios often require attention during the debugging of Nginx modules.

- Memory leaks and segmentation faults, which can be indicative of improper memory management or dereferencing null pointers.

- Handling of concurrent requests and ensuring thread-safety, particularly important for modules that maintain state or interact with external systems.

- Configuration parsing errors, where incorrect handling of directive values can lead to unexpected behavior or server startup failures.

Addressing these issues often requires a thorough understanding of Nginx's internals and the specific mechanisms by which modules integrate with the server core.

Debugging and testing Nginx modules is a multifaceted process, requiring a combination of strategic log analysis, interactive debugging, and comprehensive automated testing. By adopting a structured approach to these activities, developers can significantly improve the reliability and performance of their modules, contributing to the overall stability and efficiency of the Nginx server.

10.10   Contributing to the Nginx Community

Contributing to the Nginx community goes beyond merely developing modules or contributing code. It encompasses a wide range of activities that aim to support and enhance the Nginx ecosystem. These activities include, but are not limited to, developing modules, reporting bugs, providing patches for existing issues, writing documentation, and actively participating in community forums. In this section, we focus on the various avenues through which contributions can be made, the standard practices for such contributions, and how to effectively engage with the Nginx community.

Let's start with the process of identifying areas for contribution. Potential contributors should first familiarize themselves with the Nginx project, which involves understanding its architecture, features, and the roles of its various components. Following this, contributors can identify areas where they can add value, based on their skills and interests. These areas might include:

- Enhancements to existing features

- Bug fixes

- New features or modules

- Documentation improvements

- Community support and education

Once an area for contribution has been identified, the next step is to understand the guidelines for contributions. The Nginx community has established practices designed to maintain the quality and integrity of the project. Before starting contributions, one should review these guidelines, available on the Nginx official website or the repository's CONTRIBUTING.md file, if applicable. The guidelines cover aspects such as coding standards, commit message formats, and the process for making a pull request.

Contributing code changes or new features usually involves the following steps:

1. Fork the repository to your account.

2. Clone the forked repository to your local development environment.

3. Create a new branch for your changes.

4. Implement the changes or new features, adhering to the coding standards.

5. Write tests to validate your changes as needed.

6. Push the changes to your forked repository.

7. Submit a pull request to the main Nginx repository.

In the case of writing and testing changes, let's illustrate how to use the Nginx testing framework. When developing new features or fixing bugs, it is paramount to ensure that your changes do not introduce regressions. Nginx provides a testing framework to facilitate this. To add a test case for a new feature, you can follow this example:

```
http {
    include mime.types;
    default_type application/octet-stream;
    server {
        listen 8080;
        location / {
            # Example configuration here
        }
    }
}
```

A test case should be designed to test specific functionality and should be reproducible. After implementing the test, run the full suite of existing tests to ensure that no existing functionality is broken by your changes.

Providing thorough documentation is also a valuable form of contribution. When contributing new features or modules, ensure that comprehensive documentation is included. Documentation should cover the purpose of the feature, configurations, usage examples, and any limitations. This not only aids in the acceptance of your contribution but also ensures that end-users can effectively leverage the new functionalities provided.

The Nginx community prefers contributions that are well-documented and include tests to verify the work. Commit messages should be clear and describe what the change accomplishes. Good commit messages enable other community members to understand the purpose of the change without needing to read the full patch.

Lastly, engaging with the community through forums, mailing lists, and issue trackers is immensely beneficial. This engagement involves asking questions, answering queries from other users, providing feedback on others' contributions, and discussing future enhancements. Such interactions foster a vibrant community and drive the continual improvement of the Nginx project.

In summary, contributing to the Nginx community is a multifaceted endeavor that requires understanding both the technical and social components of the project. Effective contributions are those that are thoughtful, well-documented, rigorously tested, and in line with the project's guidelines and goals. By embracing these practices, contributors not only enhance the functionality and reliability of Nginx but also ensure its ongoing relevance in the ever-evolving landscape of web technologies.

10.11   Integrating Third-Party Modules

Integrating third-party modules into Nginx is an effective method to extend its functionality without the need to develop custom modules from scratch. This approach leverages the thriving ecosystem around Nginx, where developers contribute diverse modules that cater to various specific needs. In this section, we will discuss how to locate suitable third-party modules, how to assess their compatibility and quality, and the steps involved in integrating them into Nginx.

Locating Third-Party Modules

The first step in integrating a third-party module is locating one that fulfills your requirements. The official Nginx website and GitHub are excellent starting points for finding third-party modules. Additionally, community forums and discussions can offer insights into modules that are highly regarded and widely used.

Assessing Modules

Not all modules are created equal, and it's crucial to assess them on several facets before integration:

- **Compatibility:** Ensure the module is compatible with your version of Nginx. This information is typically available in the module's documentation.

- **Maintainability:** Evaluate if the module is actively maintained, which is a sign of reliability and future-proofing.

- **Performance:** Assess any known performance implications. Some modules might introduce a negligible overhead, while others could have a more significant impact.

- **Security:** Examine any known security vulnerabilities and the history of security updates for the module.

Integration Process

Once a module has been selected, integrating it into Nginx generally involves the following steps:

1. *Preparation:* If the module source code is not readily available, it may require cloning or downloading from a repository or website.

2. *Building Nginx with the Module:* Most third-party modules are dynamic, meaning you can load them without rebuilding

Nginx from source. However, some may require building Nginx from source with the module included. The command used typically looks like this:

```
1  ./configure --add-dynamic-module=/path/to/module
2  make
3  make install
```

3. *Configuration:* After the module is integrated, it needs to be enabled in the Nginx configuration. For dynamic modules, this involves adding a load_module directive in the Nginx configuration file (nginx.conf).

```
1  load_module modules/ngx_http_my_module.so;
```

4. *Validation:* Finally, validate the Nginx configuration and restart the web server to apply changes.

```
nginx -t
nginx -s reload
```

Best Practices for Integrating Third-Party Modules

- **Testing:** Thoroughly test the module in a development environment before deploying it in production.

- **Documentation:** Keep documentation of the modules integrated, including version numbers and configuration specifics, for future reference.

- **Community Engagement:** Participate in community discussions about the module to stay abreast of updates, security patches, and best practices.

Integrating third-party modules into Nginx allows for a highly customized and powerful web server setup. By carefully selecting and integrating modules, you can enhance the functionality and performance of Nginx to meet the unique demands of your web applications.

10.12   Future   Directions   in   Nginx Development

As Nginx continues to evolve, its development is steered toward addressing the ever-changing landscape of web technologies and the demands of its diverse user base. The focus on performance, flexibility, and security remains paramount, with several key areas identified as critical for future development.

- **Enhanced Support for HTTP/3:** As the latest version of the HTTP protocol, HTTP/3 offers significant improvements in performance, particularly in reducing latency and better handling of packet loss. Future versions of Nginx will likely include greater support for HTTP/3, making it easier for developers to leverage these benefits in their applications.

- **Improved Automation and Configuration Management:** As infrastructure as code (IaC) practices gain popularity, there is a need for Nginx to integrate more seamlessly with automation tools. Enhancements in API support for configuration management and provisioning could reduce the complexity and time needed to deploy and manage Nginx instances.

- **Advanced Security Features:** Security concerns continue to be at the forefront of web development. Future Nginx versions may introduce more robust security features, such as automated SSL/TLS certificate management, enhanced DDoS mitigation, and better integration with third-party security tools.

- **Edge Computing and IoT Support:** The rise of edge computing and the Internet of Things (IoT) presents new challenges and opportunities. Nginx could play a crucial role in these environments by providing lightweight, high-performance web serving, and proxying capabilities closer to the edge, thereby reducing latency and improving data processing times.

From a module development perspective, several advancements are anticipated:

- **Streamlined Module Development:** Simplifying the process of developing custom Nginx modules can encourage more developers to extend Nginx functionality. This could involve better documentation, more accessible development tools, and a standardized API for interacting with Nginx internals.

- **Increasing Extensibility:** Enhancing the ways in which modules can interact with and modify Nginx's core processing phases could unlock new possibilities for customization and optimization.

- **Community-Driven Module Repository:** Establishing a centralized repository for third-party Nginx modules, akin to npm for Node.js or PyPI for Python, could foster a stronger community and make it easier to discover and integrate modules.

Lastly, considering the wider ecosystem and community involvement, efforts to engage more directly with users and developers through forums, hackathons, and contributions to the open-source project can nurture the growth of the Nginx ecosystem. As web technologies continue to advance, fostering a collaborative and innovative environment is essential for Nginx to remain a leader in web server technology.

The trajectory of Nginx development clearly shows a robust platform that not only adapts to current web and network technologies but also shapes future trends in the internet infrastructure landscape. By focusing on these key areas, Nginx is well-positioned to continue its legacy as a high-performance, scalable, and secure web server for years to come.

www.ingramcontent.com/pod-product-compliance
Lightning Source LLC
LaVergne TN
LVHW051438050326
832903LV00030BD/3149